Vasanta

Vasanta

Stories from Sanskrit Plays

Retold by

Arshia Sattar

JUGGERNAUT BOOKS
C-I-128, First Floor, Sangam Vihar, Near Holi Chowk,
New Delhi 110080, India

First published by Juggernaut Books 2024

10 9 8 7 6 5 4 3 2 1

P-ISBN: 978-93-5345-413-5
E-ISBN: 978-93-5345-440-1

Typeset in Arno Pro by R. Ajith Kumar, Noida

Printed at Replika Press Pvt. Ltd.

Contents

An Historical Introduction

Ancient India has bequeathed to the world an amazing storehouse of engaging stories, narrated through drama, prose and poetry. This historical introduction offers readers some broad brushstrokes to provide historical contexts for the stories recounted in this book.* Of course the stories can be enjoyed for their own sake. But embedding them in history encourages us to ask questions such as: What do the characters, plots and ideas in these stories tell us about times long past? What was the background of the creators of these stories? Who were their patrons and audiences? To what extent did subordinate and marginalized social groups –lower classes and castes, women, tribal people – participate in literary culture? What was the connection between literature and politics? Were there links between 'high' literature and popular culture? Why were some stories told, retold and enjoyed over the centuries in many different ways, in different languages, in written, oral, visual and performative forms, while others fell by the wayside and were forgotten?

To make sense of what was going on in India in the first millennium, we need to backtrack to the sixth/fifth century BCE,

* For further details, see Upinder Singh, *A History of Ancient and Early Medieval India*, 2nd edition (New Delhi, Pearson, 2024).

one of the most exciting periods in Indian history. In North India, this was a period of warring states. Monarchies and oligarchies made military and matrimonial alliances and battled each other in their quest for political gain. The emergence and growth of cities ushered in new ways of living and thinking. The origins of the caste system, based on endogamy and hereditary occupation, go back to this period. In Brahminical texts, the Brahmin was placed at the top of the social ladder, the 'untouchable' at the bottom. It is not a coincidence that a time of escalating violence and rapid social change was also a time when thinkers like Mahavira and the Buddha questioned the authority of Brahmins, emphasized the importance of social ethics and preached doctrines of nonviolence and detachment. Jainism and Buddhism asserted the superiority of Kshatriyas over Brahmins, but held that the truly superior person was one who had attained mastery over the senses and freedom from the cycle of birth and death. We should remember that while some people lived in towns and cities, most people lived in the rural countryside, and vast swathes of land across the subcontinent were inhabited by forest tribes who had their own cultural traditions and ways of life.

The rise of the kingdom of Magadha began in the 6th century BCE under the Haryanka and Shaishunaga dynasties, continued under the Nandas and reached a high point under the Mauryas (c. 324/321–187 BCE). The first two Maurya kings – Chandragupta and Bindusara – fought the wars that led to the creation of an empire that eventually extended (in in an uneven way) over almost the entire subcontinent (except the far south), and into Afghanistan in the northwest. Pataliputra was its capital. The third Maurya king, Ashoka, is famous for renouncing war and devoting himself to a vigorous propagation of *dhamma* (the Prakrit form of *dharma*). This was a code of ethics he designed; it was rooted in, but not identical to, Buddhism. Ashoka's dhamma can be understood as goodness, measured in terms of inner qualities as well as external behaviour, towards people as well as animals. The emperor put in place an elaborate propaganda machinery for the dissemination of dhamma. He ordered its tenets inscribed on rocks and pillars and exhorted his officials to spread the teaching. He himself spent a great deal of time travelling around his empire, trying to convince his subjects to be good. Power seems to have gone to his head and he formed an exaggerated idea of the success of his dhamma campaign. The Maurya dynasty came to an end due to a military coup, when Pushyamitra Shunga, the Brahmin commander-in-chief, killed the last Maurya king, Brihaḍratha, during a military review, grabbed the reins of power and established the Shunga dynasty. The rule of the Shungas was followed by that of the Mitras and Kanvas.

Empires usually advertise themselves well and hence attract a great deal of popular and scholarly attention and interest. The period c. 200 BCE to 300 CE, sandwiched between the Maurya and Gupta empires, used to be seen as a bleak, dark age. Not anymore. These five centuries were momentous from many points of view. State formation spread to various parts of the subcontinent. The porous northern frontier of the Hindu Kush mountains was breached repeatedly by waves of invaders – Bactrian Greeks, Shakas, Parthians and Kushanas. The Satavahanas emerged as a major political force in the western Deccan and fought with the Shaka Kshatrapas for control over the trade routes and ports of western India. In the far south, the Chola, Chera and Pandya kings ruled in the midst of many chieftains. Old cities expanded and new ones emerged all over the subcontinent. Cities hummed with cultural and intellectual activity. Craftspersons produced larger quantities and more varied goods than before. Routes over land and water criss-crossed the various regions of the subcontinent and connected it with distant lands, from the Mediterranean to Southeast Asia. Kings issued coins made of precious metals as well as base metals and alloys. These often had portraits of rulers and deities and writing on them, and functioned both as a medium of economic exchange and political messaging. Many new cultural winds blew into the subcontinent, especially the northwest, in the wake of invasions and expanding trade. Sophisticated styles of stone sculpture emerged in Gandhara and Mathura and coexisted with the older traditions of terracotta art. The devotional worship of images of deities in shrines became a cornerstone of religious life. The emergence of Mahayana Buddhism, the split in the Jaina sangha (monastic order) between the Digambaras and Shvetambaras and the growing popularity of Vaishnavism, Shaivism and Shaktism are important aspects of the religious history of these centuries.

Vedic hymns and the Sanskrit epics (Mahabharata and Ramayana) contain literary elements, but something that we can recognize as full-fledged literature was born at the cusp of the new millennium. It was born in three languages – Sanskrit, Prakrit and Tamil. Ashvaghosha and Bhasa were the earliest known exponents of Sanskrit *kavya* (literature). The Satavahana king, Hala, is said to have been a poet and a complier of the *Gatha Sattasai*, an anthology of fine Prakrit poetry. Kings and chieftains of South India patronized poets who composed poems of love and war in Tamil, later collected into the anthologies *Ettutokai* and *Pattupattu*. Rulers were not the only patrons or audiences of literature. The urban connoisseurs with a taste for the fine things in life included businessmen, merchants and sophisticated courtesans referred to in Sanskrit texts as *ganikas*. The creation and consumption of literature was very much an urban phenomenon.

Sanskrit rapidly acquired prestige as a premier language for religious, intellectual and literary expression. It also started taking over from Prakrit as the language of political power. Kings started proclaiming their authority through their *prashastis* in inscriptions: a section of a royal inscription, and sometimes the entire inscription, was devoted to the king's praise. The prashastis gave details of genealogies and political events and generally reported political successes rather than defeats. They advertised the greatness of kings on and off the battlefield, presenting them in a flattering light in increasingly sophisticated literary prose and verse. Kings started issuing land grants with tax benefits to Brahmins and Buddhist monasteries. These were recorded on stone or copper plates and provide valuable information about changes taking place in political, social and economic life. The beneficiaries of these land grants were not necessarily directly aligned with rulers' personal religious beliefs. For instance, the Satavahana rulers, who were Brahmins and performers of Vedic sacrifices, made generous grants to Buddhist monks. The general strategy, which was politically astute, was to build alliances with Brahmins and with different kinds of burgeoning religious institutions.

It was not only kings who were developing the epigraphic habit. Ordinary people had their religious devotion inscribed in hundreds of donative inscriptions across the subcontinent. These include inscriptions at Buddhist sites such as Sanchi and Bharhut in Central India and Nashik, Karle and other cave sites in the Western Ghats. In South India, there are hundreds of inscriptions in the Tamil language and Tamil–Brahmi script, many of them recording donations to the Jain monastic order. Donative inscriptions offer exciting glimpses into social history and tell us about the background of the people who were funding the religious establishments that were mushrooming all over the subcontinent. For instance, inscriptions from the western Deccan mention jewellers, goldsmiths, blacksmiths, ironmongers, perfumers and stone masons as donors.

The period c. 300–600 CE is often referred to as 'the Gupta period', but we should remember that while the Gupta dynasty extended its sway over parts of North and Central India, the Vakataka dynasty was powerful in the western Deccan, and many other less powerful kings and chieftains ruled in other parts of the subcontinent. In South India, the Pallavas came to power towards the end of this period. The Guptas and Vakatakas were connected with each other through a matrimonial alliance. The Gupta princess Prabhavatigupta was married to the Vakataka Rudrasena II and, after the latter's death, she wielded power for many years as queen regent. It was not entirely a man's world.

In the first half of the 20th century, historians writing against the background of the nationalist movement, often described the rule of the Gupta dynasty as ushering a 'golden age' marked by political unification, economic prosperity and achievements in the fields of literature, art and architecture. During the 1960's and 1970s, this was replaced by a more dispassionate view and a better understanding of the complexities of the Gupta empire. Gupta kings are known from their inscriptions, fine gold coins and seals. Their inscriptions include the famous one inscribed on a pillar located in the precincts of the fort at Allahabad, now known as Prayagraj, which proclaims the greatness of Samudragupta (c. 350–370 CE). Interestingly, this pillar also bears Ashokan inscriptions and an inscription of the Mughal emperor Jahangir! Samudragupta's inscription, composed by a high-ranking officer named Harishena, describes the king's military achievements in great detail, in exceptionally fine Sanskrit verse and prose. It also advertises his many virtues and talents, including as a musician, a role in which he is portrayed on some of his gold coins. The Gupta empire declined in the wake of competition from the Vakatakas, the rise of King Yashodharman of Malwa and the invasions of the Hunas from Central Asia.

Even if we abandon the longing for golden ages, there is no doubt that the period c. 300–600 CE saw the production of an exceptionally fine range of literature and the compilation of a great variety kinds of texts. The great Sanskrit litterateurs of the period included Kalidasa, Vishakhadatta, Shudraka, Bharavi and Subandhu. It is interesting that the flowering of Sanskrit kavya took place at a time when Sanskrit had long ceased to be a language spoken by ordinary people. This is reflected in the fact that Sanskrit drama is actually bilingual. With some exceptions, kings and upper-class men speak Sanskrit, while women and lower-class men speak a Prakrit dialect. While the plays represent the perspectives of the socially privileged, they also have elements of social and political critique and satire, often voiced by the *vidushaka,* the hero's Brahmin companion, who tends to speak his mind and provides welcome comic relief.

During the period c. 300–600 CE, the Mahabharata and Ramayana and the major Puranas were given final shape. Several Dharmashastra texts belong to this period; so does the famous treatise on pleasure, the *Kama Sutra*. Works on politics included the *Nitisara* and the *Panchatantra*. Major advances were made in medicine, astronomy and mathematics. All this could not have been possible without the patronage of affluent urban people. The basic plan of the early Hindu temple was laid in the Gupta period, but in terms of spectacular remains, the most striking ones are the Buddhist Ajanta caves. These caves, with their exquisite mural paintings and sculptures, lay in the Vakataka kingdom and were mainly patronized by high-ranking ministers during the reign of King Harishena.

Historians often use the term 'early medieval' for the period between c. 600 and 1200 CE. History is full of lively debates. In the older history books, these centuries used to be described as marked by crisis, decline, decay and decadence. Some historians saw this as the result of the Ghaznavid and Ghurid invasions and the advent of Muslim rulers in North India. These perspectives were challenged by historians who argued that the early medieval period was marked by feudalism in the political and rural spheres due to royal land grants, and a decline in city life, trade and the use of money. And then *this* theory was questioned by historians who argued that during the early medieval period, state formation spread to various new parts of the subcontinent and that various integrative processes were at work; that there were changes in urban centres, trade and coined money, but no overall decline. In fact, there are many continuities with developments in previous centuries. The practice of making royal land grants, which began much earlier, became more widespread and intensive. Kings sought to legitimate their power by making land grants and this led to the emergence of Brahmins as a powerful landed class. Temples too benefitted from the generosity of kings and upwardly mobile social groups such as merchants. The caste system spread to more areas. Several tribal communities came under Brahminical influence and were absorbed into its lower rungs.

This was a time of great vitality in the intellectual, creative and artistic fields. Important changes were in the air. Sheldon Pollock suggests that there were two great moments of transformation in culture and power in pre-modern India.* Around the beginning of the Common Era, Sanskrit, which had a long history as a sacred language in the sphere of religion and ritual, started being used in literary and political expression. Sanskrit texts and the ideas they contained spread far beyond the subcontinent. Then, around the beginning of the second millennium CE, regional languages challenged the position of Sanskrit in the spheres of literature and power, and eventually replaced it. This was connected with the increasingly regional flavour of politics and culture.

A wide range of texts in different languages were written in the early medieval period. The most famous names in Sanskrit literature include Banabhatta, Magha, Bhavabhuti, Dandin and Shriharsha. Although women characters are important in Sanskrit literature, women writers are rare. Works on poetics mention poetesses and cite some of their verses, but the only complete work that seems to have been written by a woman is a play called *Kaumudimahotsava,* attributed to a Chalukya queen named Vijjika. The many Sanskrit texts on literary theory, poetics and aesthetics written during early medieval times include works by Dandin, Vamana, Anandavardhana, Rudrata, Rajashekhara, Mammata, Abhinavagupta and Bhoja. Other types of Sanskrit texts included philosophical commentaries, religious texts, story literature and works on technical subjects such as grammar, lexicography, poetics, dramaturgy, music, architecture, medicine

* Sheldon Pollock, *The Language of the Gods in the World of Men: Sanskrit, Culture and Power in Premodern India* (Delhi: Permanent Black [2006] 2007).

and mathematics. Tamil literature flourished and includes the beautiful songs of the Vaishnava and Shaiva saints known as the Alvars and Nayanmars, and Kamban's *Iramavataram*, a Tamil rendering of Rama's story. We also see the beginnings of Kannada and Telugu literature. Writers and intellectuals wrote on different subjects and could be fluent in several languages. For instance, Dandin's native language was Tamil, but he wrote the *Dashakumaracharita* ('Tale of Ten Princes') and *Kavyadarsha*, a book on poetics, in Sanskrit. The latter circulated widely and was translated into many languages including Tamil, Kannada, Sinhala and Tibetan. So ideas and creativity flowed freely thanks to multi-lingualism and translation.

The many kings of the early medieval period included Harshavardhana of the Pushyabhuti dynasty, who ruled in the 7th century. He is largely known from the *Harshacharita*, a prose biography written by his court poet, Banabhatta, and the account of the Chinese traveller-monk, Xuanzang. The Pushyabhutis initially had their base in the area around Sthanishvara (modern Thanesar in Ambala district, Punjab). They forged a marriage alliance with the Maukharis of Kanyakubja (Kannauj). After the death of the Maukhari ruler, Grahavarman, Kannauj passed into the hands of the Pushyabhutis. Xuanzang gives a vivid description of the beauty, grandeur and prosperity of Kannauj. Harsha was a patron of learning and the arts. Bana, Mayura and Matanga Divakara were among the accomplished writers who adorned his court. The king himself was a scholar and writer and is supposed to have written three dramas – the *Ratnavali*, *Priyadarshika* and *Nagananda*. It is possible that he composed the text of the Banskhera and Madhuban inscriptions. The former has the king's signature!

One of the important features of the early medieval period was the rise of various Rajput lineages and a struggle for power between the Gurjara-Pratiharas, Palas and Rashtrakutas. The political history of South India was dominated by the Pallavas, Pandyas, Cheras and Cholas. Inscriptions refer to early kings of the Pallava line who ruled in the early 4th century, but the great Pallava political expansion really took off towards the end of the 6th century under Simhavishnu, who conquered the land up to the Kaveri. The Pallavas ruled over Tondaimandalam, the land between the north Pennar and Vellar rivers, with their capital at Kanchipuram. They were embroiled in conflicts with the Western Chalukyas, Rashtrakutas, Pandyas and rulers of Sri Lanka. In the late 9th century, control over Tondaimandalam passed into the hands of the Cholas. The Chola empire reached its heights during the time of Rajaraja I. The reign of Rajaraja's son, Rajendra, saw a Chola naval expedition against the kingdom of Srivijaya (located on the island of Sumatra). Usually, men occupied the throne. But women of the royal household wielded power and authority, and there are some instances of queens ruling in their own right. Three instances come from Kashmir – Didda, Yashovati and Sugandha. While history books are full of details of battles between kings of various dynasties, hundreds of hero stones found all over the country celebrate unnamed heroes and bear silent testimony to the pervasiveness of different kinds of conflict and violence at the local level.

Agrarian expansion continued in various parts of the subcontinent. Social and economic distinctions within rural societies became more marked. Some of this was connected with the phenomenon of royal land grants, already mentioned above. Urban crafts, cities and trade and trade guilds flourished.

Inscriptions mention several commodities involved in trade transactions, for instance rice, pulses, sesame, salt, pepper, oil, cloth, betel leaf, areca nut and metals. The market towns and ports of South India participated in a flourishing subcontinental trade as well as long-distance maritime trade. Powerful merchant guilds such as the Ayyavole and Manigramam played an important role in long distance trade in staples as well as luxury goods. Trade links between the Indian subcontinent, Central Asia, China and Southeast Asia expanded significantly. Many ships docked at the ports on the eastern coast. Mamallapuram developed under the Pallavas, while Nagapattinam rose to prominence under the Cholas.

The Pallava kings, especially Mahendravarman I, Narasimhavarman I and Narasimhavarman II Rajasimha, were great patrons of the arts. Mahendravarman was also a writer. He is said to be the author of the *Mattavilasa-prahasana,* a rollicking satire, which makes fun of all sorts of religious people. Under the Pallavas, Tamil started being used in royal inscriptions. Initially, there was a division of labour between Sanskrit and Tamil, with Sanskrit used for the royal eulogy portion and Tamil for the details of the grant. This trend continued for quite some time.

The history of stone architecture in South India begins in the 7th century and can be connected with the increasing popularity of the bhakti sects. The remains of Pallava period architecture and sculpture are mostly found at Mahabalipuram (Mamallapuram) and Kanchipuram. There are cave temples, monolithic temples and structural temples. The most magnificent accomplishment of the artists and sculptors of the Pallava kingdom is the gigantic open-air relief at Mahabalipuram, interpreted either as representing the story of Arjuna's penance before receiving the Pashupata weapon from Shiva; or Bhagiratha's penance which led to the Ganga River descending to earth but only after the powerful impact of its flow was broken by Shiva's locks. Perhaps the artists deliberately sought to convey ambiguity and mystery. The great architectural remains of the Chola period are found further south. The Brihadishvara temple marks the culmination of Chola architecture and is an example of a temple with important political significance. The Chola period is also known for the technical and aesthetic finesse of the bronzes produced by its artisans, especially those depicting Shiva as Nataraja (Lord of Dance).

Many of the most magnificent Indian temples were built in the early medieval period. Temples were of course sacred spaces, but they were more. Some became important parts of the urban landscape, others became symbols of political power. They attracted patronage from a wide variety of social groups, ranging from kings to merchants. There was an efflorescence and refinement in temple architecture and sculpture, and distinct regional styles emerged. The Arab invasion of Sind in the 8th century and the active role of the Arabs in Indian Ocean trade led to the advent of Islam in the subcontinent. From the 11th century onwards, during the rule of the Delhi Sultans, Islam and the Persian language played an increasingly important role in Indian history. Remains of the earliest mosques in the subcontinent go back to the 8th century and are found in Sindh, Kutch and Gwalior. Christian, Jewish and Zoroastrian settlers made their homes in India, especially along the western coast. Islam, Christianity, Judaism and Zoroastrianism originated in other parts of Asia, but during the early medieval period, they became part of Indian history.

Across the centuries, the Indian subcontinent was both an area of cultural influence as well as confluence. People, texts and ideas travelled. Many ancient Indian texts such as the Mahabharata, the Ramayana, the *Arthasastra,* the *Manu Smriti* and the *Nitisara* travelled extensively and were known in Southeast Asia. Literature and stories travelled. The works of Kalidasa, Bharavi, Bana and Mayura were known in Southeast Asia. The Jataka stories travelled along with Buddhism to various parts of Asia and were narrated through words and images in texts and sculptures. The *Panchatantra,* with its hard-headed lessons on politics and sensible living told through animal stories, travelled even more widely. The earliest translations were into Pahlavi and Arabic, but many more followed, the characters sometimes being replaced by those more familiar to the translators. In India, *Panchatantra* stories were incorporated into later anthologies. They also seem to have influenced the Arabian Nights, the fables of La Fontaine and Sufi mystic literature. There are many beautifully illustrated Persian and Arabic manuscripts of the *Panchatantra*. Throughout history, stories have been told in many different ways, through spoken and written words, images and performances. Whatever may be the form, the world loves a good story!

Literature is not just a backdrop to history; it is an important *part* of history. The voices of ancient poets and writers that have survived across the centuries are precious expressions of imaginative creativity, evocations of a time long gone. Some of the stories, and they *ways* in which they are told, continue to enchant and enthral, even after centuries, even if we read them in translation, even if we may read different meanings into them today.

Upinder Singh
Professor of History
Ashoka University

Why I Like Sanskrit Plays

The plays in this selection of retellings are chosen from the works of the major Sanskrit dramatists, from Bhasa to Shudraka. They cover nearly a millennium – from the second century CE to the ninth century CE – and were written mostly in the northern regions of the Indian subcontinent. Unlike dramatic works in other classical languages (such as Tamil), much of Sanskrit drama from this period and this region has survived, giving us a veritable feast of styles and genres, a multitude of reasons to laugh and cry as we engage with the human situations and emotions that play out before our eyes.

Like the classical period in Greece, drama was a major part of Sanskrit culture. But unlike in Greece, we know little about when and how Sanskrit plays were performed. From other Sanskrit sources, we surmise that plays were performed on significant occasions such as royal coronations and at the great sacrifices that kings conducted. Since all Sanskrit plays open with an invocation to the gods (usually Shiva), we can assume that the plays also had a specifically ritual aspect and were probably performed in temple precincts or other sacred spaces. Every play is first offered to the gods by the *sutradhar,* a combination of what we could call the director and the stage manager, who asks for their blessings to ensure a flawless performance. After that, he turns to the audience, inviting them into the play, as it were, and begs their indulgence for any errors that might occur.

We know these performance conventions from the *Natya Shastra*, a text attributed to the sage Bharata and probably compiled at the turn of the first millennium. In six thousand verses, it lays out, among other things, detailed rules for writing plays and for performing them, for the training of actors and for the dimensions and requirements for the stage. Performance areas were bare, with actors indicating through movement and gesture the different locations and spaces in which the action occurred. Singing and dancing were a part of dramatic performance and so, actors needed to have many skills. But because the *Natya Shastra* is a prescriptive manual, it tells us how a performance should be and not how it was – for this reason, we have very little concrete information about how plays were actually performed.

While we do not know much about audiences and where and how the plays were performed in their own time, their stories and emotions do not feel unfamiliar. We may think of Sanskrit language and culture as far away, in a past that we cannot recapture, but many of the dramatic conventions established in Sanskrit plays continue in our folk theatres today, even in the mainstream films that we watch – the noble hero, the innocent heroine, the bumbling but lovable fool, the happy ending where all the loose ends are tied up in a neat knot. Their stories, too, make us feel as if we have heard or read them before.

Despite these resonances, the world of Sanskrit plays can nonetheless seem alienating to us. For example, it does not on the whole, produce unique characters remembered for a tragic flaw or a great speech. In fact, as modern readers, we might initially feel a sense of frustration with the lack of psychological depth to the characters. Where are the internal monologues, the soliloquies? How do we access their minds and their motivations? Even in their courtships and flirtations they seem to be playing at love, enacting its moods according to a complex set of conventions and rules, rather than succumbing to the throes of passion and desire.

We can also get lost in the profusion of characters, all of them with long and complicated names, who are not distinguished by feature or function. Characters such as the heroine's girlfriends or the young women in the queen's retinue, for example, are the same across plays and situations. They are necessary as they deliver letters and messages and move the plot along in various ways, often by divulging critical information or overhearing secret conversations which they promptly share with their friends and, often, with their mistresses. But Priyamvada could be replaced by Chaturika and we might not even notice.

Why, then, should we read these plays at all? One way to experience the pleasures that Sanskrit plays afford might be to consider what they ask of their audiences, in this case, their reader. Sanskrit drama lays great emphasis on the *sahridaya,* the worthy spectator, who is able to receive fully all the intentions and the emotions with which the writer has imbued the play. This sahridaya, a person of 'like-heartedness', must be well-educated and well-informed, an aesthete, one who understands not only Sanskrit and the other verbal languages of the play, but also the languages of movement and gesture.

I would suggest that the like-hearted person has other virtues they might bring with them to their spectatorship: one of them would be prior knowledge of the stories that the plays draw from. This kind of sahridaya is able to feel more intensely for the characters in the plays because they have already been sympathetic to them in previous versions of the story. The playwright counts on the fact that the sahridaya already knows the stories – whether it be Bhasa or Bhavabhuti, whose plays are so firmly rooted in the Ramayana and the Mahabharata, or Harsha who assumes a knowledge of Udayana's adventures and the conquest of his many wives. Some readers of this book may be familiar with a few of the stories and that would certainly give them the added pleasure of experiencing them retold.

Our hearts go out to Shakuntala, the gentle child of the forest, when she comes to reclaim the promise of marriage from the king who had seduced her. If we have known her before from the Mahabharata, we have previously suffered with her through this public humiliation and when we encounter her in Kalidasa's *Abhijnanashakuntalam* ('Shakuntala'), our sympathy for her is intensified. Vishakhadatta calls upon the well-known legend of Chanakya and his strategic manipulations that stabilized the early days of Chandragupta Maurya's reign. As a result, we admire Chanakya anew in *Mudrarakshasa* ('The Minister's Signet Ring'). Even Shudraka, who invents a plot for *Mricchakatika* ('The Little Clay Cart'), litters his play with references to incidents and characters from the epics. Samsthanaka is established as an illiterate buffoon precisely because he constantly misquotes the epics and confuses their main characters with each other. Someone who knows the epics can appreciate the extent of Samsthanaka's boorishness and be amused by it.

The pleasure we take in these plays lies in the fact they tell us the old stories in new and different ways, deepening our acquaintance with literary characters and bringing us closer to them as we re-live their trials and triumphs and share their emotions. However, even if we are reading the stories for the first time, I believe they have enough charm and whimsy to hold our attention.

In choosing the plays for this book, I have mostly avoided those that retell or invent episodes for the Ramayana and the Mahabharata, even though they are some of the best among those that constitute 'classical' Sanskrit drama. We are familiar with what happens to Rama and Sita and to the main characters in the Mahabharata – Sanskrit epic plays simply expand these narrative arcs, often with great insight and sensitivity. I made the decision to put those plays aside because I wanted to focus on the stories that Sanskrit playwrights chose from other sources, to indicate the variety and breadth of landscapes and moods that they chose to explore in their dramatic works.

For example, *Malavikagnimitram* ('Malavika and Agnimitra'), which is widely held to be Kalidasa's first play, has a historical source, based on the establishment and the expansion of the Sunga empire that flourished in northern India for about a century around 180 CE. So also, Bhasa's *Pratijna Yaugandharayana* ('Yaugandharayana's Vow') revolves around the exploits of a possibly historical ruler, King Udayana, who might have been a contemporary of Gautama Buddha. We have already remarked on how 'The Minister's Signet Ring' too, finds its inspiration in the legend of Chanakya's dedicated service to his young king, Chandragupta Maurya. Whether or not Chanakya was a historical figure, Chandragupta certainly was.

Stories from the secular narrative traditions also find their way into the canon of Sanskrit drama. Harsha's *Ratnavali* ('The Lady with the Garland of Jewels') takes its its story from the *Kathasaritsagara*, Somadeva's compilation of tales that had criss-crossed the sub-continent like rivers, carrying adventure, intrigue and magic. Other Sanskrit playwrights (such as Bhasa), also used these stories. Of course, they were writing centuries before Somadeva put his text together. Their source was probably an older, lost text – the *Brihatkatha,* which predates the *Sagara* by at least five or six hundred years.

As we seek the sources of the stories that these plays (re)tell, we find ourselves in a wonderfully Borgesian predicament: we are looking for a story from a lost (or perhaps, actually non-existent but presumed) source, the *Brihatkatha,* to fully understand and fill out a story that we have (the one in the play). In order to find that earlier story so we understand the one we have better, we refer to a version that is a later telling, from the *Kathasaritsagara,* than the one we are trying to authenticate.

What a conundrum – because no story in the subcontinent is ever lost or completely forgotten, the labyrinthine intertextuality of our storytelling never fails to boggle the mind. But it also shows us, time and again, that the story teller is a hard working person, well-read and well-informed of all that has been told before and even, with mysterious foresight, what will be told after.

The phenomenon of intertextuality shows itself when texts across time as well as contemporaneously know each other and refer to each other, when they seem to be in conversation with each other. Story texts don't 'talk' only to other story texts. The period between the second and fourth centuries CE was a time when many ideas and doctrines were compiled, redacted and 'stabilized', . The Dharma Shastras came together and coalesced around an increasingly dominant version, the *Manu Smriti*. So, too, single texts with putative individual authors, such as Kautilya's *Arthashastra* and Vatsyayana's *Kama Sutra,* developed, reflecting the concerns of a social and political structure that was both urban and imperial.

'The Minister's Signet Ring' and the plays in which Yaugandharayana appears are all about wise (and wily) ministers who keep their kings secure on the throne. But they also give us a sense of what was actually happening in the world they wrote about. Palace intrigues and conspiracies against kings were common, there were frequent skirmishes at the borders of kingdoms as local rulers and oligarchs nibbled at the edges of larger imperial formations, political alliances were made as often through marriages as they were through diplomacy or force. Royal courts were complicated eco-systems with what seems like hundreds of retainers and courtiers and officials and ministers who had informants and spy rings, and all of whom were connected and dependent on each other.

The *Arthashastra* was likely to have informed the writing of these plays and determined the ways in which the characters of the ministers were drawn in terms of their temperaments and actions. 'The Little Clay Cart's' Vasantasena is most certainly the perfect courtesan as imagined in the *Kama Sutra* and her impecunious lover, Charudatta, displays the refined tastes and pleasures of the text's sophisticated, wealthy man-about-town, worthy partner to the courtesan who is trained in all the sixty-four arts.

The hierarchies of the Dharma Shastras are implicit in the texts and plots of Sanskrit plays and reflect the fact that caste was an operative factor in real-life social interactions. Moreover, the aesthetic rules that govern the writing of plays reinforce these hierarchies and divisions: the hero of a *nataka*, for example, must be high born and the woman he falls in love with must be equal to him in status. Hence, the forest girl must actually be the daughter of a kshatriya and the palace maid who catches the king's eye is a princess in disguise for her own safety.

The Dharma Shastras also make a more emphatic appearance in some scenes where caste is overtly referred to. In 'The Little Clay Cart', the captain of the king's guard and a soldier get into a squabble about whether or not a carriage has been appropriately inspected. The captain, who has covered up the identity of the passenger in the carriage, needs to make sure that the soldier will not make his own inspection and so, he picks a fight with him, accusing him of being from a family of low caste barbers. The soldier responds by reminding his superior in rank that he, too, has low caste origins, as he is a tanner who deals with the skins of dead animals. While no caste names are mentioned, the social status of both men is clear in the insults that they throw at one another. Later in the play, when Charudatta is being led to his execution, his great shame lies in the fact that the false accusations against him have sullied his personal and his caste (brahmin) reputation. In 'The Minister's Signet Ring', the deposed minister of the previous regime frets that the new king, Chandragupta, is low caste.

I enjoy these plays because I know the stories they tell and the texts they reference. However, I don't only like them because I know them twice over. I also like them because they show us a vibrant and diverse cultural past, they tell us about cities like the ones we live in, they suggest that the men who ruled supported the arts and promoted a culture of tolerance and co-existence.

Harshavardhana, the author of 'The Lady with the Garland of Jewels' and 'Nagananda', ruled from Kannauj, located in the great river plain of Ganga in the early seventh century CE. We know from other contemporaneous sources that Harsha was a Shaivite, but the Chinese pilgrim and scholar, Xuanzang, who visited Kannauj during his reign, describes him as a devout Buddhist. Harsha was a contemporary of the mighty Pallava monarch, Mahendravarman whose kingdom covered the central part of the southern plateau in the sub-continent. Mahendravarman, who was probably a Jain before he became a Shaivite, was a scholar, a painter, a musician and an architect. He also wrote at least one play, a satire called *Mattavilasa.* During his reign, another Sanskrit comedy, *Bhagavadajjukiya* ('The Holy Man and the Courtesan') was written by Bodhayana, but the play is often credited to Mahendravarman himself.

Whatever the personal beliefs of these kings might have been, the plays they wrote (or the plays that are attributed to them in panegyrics by their loyal court poets) certainly have a distance from orthodox Hindu beliefs and practice. The records we have of their reigns also indicate a healthy eclecticism towards the diverse religious and sectarian ideas that clearly prevailed in the first millennium.

How casually it is mentioned that kings were playwrights! Or, if you prefer it the other way, that playwrights were kings. In addition to Harsha and Mahendravarman, Shudraka might also have been a king. The prologue to his 'The Little Clay Cart' tells us that the playwright was a wise ruler who had performed the *ashwamedha* sacrifice to establish his regional supremacy and that he was known as 'Shudraka'. Some scholars suggest that Shudraka was an Abhira ruler from the third century CE, while some others place him earlier, as a Satavahana monarch of the second century CE. Perhaps coincidentally, all three of these playwright-kings have left us with *a-pauranika* plays, that is, plays whose stories are not drawn from Hindu epics or mythologies. The plots of their plays are putatively historical or original or are taken from secular texts like *Brihatkatha.*

Despite the evidence of these diverse and fluid beliefs and practices, we tend to think of classical Sanskrit as a handmaiden primarily to Hindu religion and culture. But as Sheldon Pollock has persuasively shown us, over the centuries, Sanskrit had become a vehicle to express political and cultural power and was used by all kinds of people. Whatever other languages they might have used (such as Pali and various Prakrits), Buddhists, Jains and other less mainstream religious and philosophical groups (such as the Materialists) also used Sanskrit as a dynamic receptacle of their political beliefs and religious ideas. Just as an example, the first extant Sanskrit play we have was written by Ashvaghosha, a Buddhist. In the *Buddhacharita,* Ashvaghosha writes a grand narrative of Gautama Buddha's life and expounds the central ideas of the Buddhist creed. Clearly, in the classical period and after, Sanskrit writing went beyond the universe of Hindu ideas and practices, in drama as well as other kinds of literature.

This kind of historical information and context only corroborates what we experience when we read the plays, for they themselves point to the pluralistic cultures that birthed them. They speak of distant wars, of shipwrecks and travellers, they imagine a vast world of known and unknown places that lie well beyond the locale of the play and that contribute to its plot. Almost all Sanskrit plays were written in and around royal courts and were intended for social elites, so we find that the action of the plays, too, takes place in these familiar surrounds. Since the royal courts were located in cities, the pulsating energies that drive the plays are actually the cities themselves. Cities thrived because of the presence of the merchants and traders who helped build and sustain them. We know that by the cusp of the first millennium, trade was dominated by Buddhists and Jains. It should be no surprise, then, that Buddhists and Jains might also have made contributions to the universe of classical Sanskrit drama: as playwrights, patrons and audiences.

Cities were spaces of religious and cultural diversity even when their kings and ruling elites were demonstrably Hindu, Buddhist or Jain. Their easy pluralism is manifest, for example, in the frequent appearances of characters such as Buddhist nuns who are treated with great respect as women of virtue and wisdom. Buddhist ideas are often appreciated – brahmins, in the form of the *vidushaka* , are figures of fun; renunciants and ascetics are both admired and mocked; Tantrics and other marginal Hindu sects, such as the Kapalakas, lurk on the fringes of many stories and, in 'Malati and Madhava', become crucial to the plot. In *Ratnavali*, the Simhala princess in disguise is curious about how the people celebrate the Spring festival as it is sure to be different from the way it is celebrated in her country.

Possibly, the most compelling portrait of an ancient cosmopolis where people from different castes, occupations and religions mingled freely is in 'The Little Clay Cart'. Set in Ujjain, the play fully exploits this diversity of peoples and professions for its action – its heroic characters are a masseur, a thief and a shepherd who leads a people's revolution against a corrupt king. A courtesan – and not a chaste virgin – is the play's central female character. She remains an object of sexual desire but is also much admired and praised for her kindness and generosity.

So, I love these plays because I am thrilled when characters go against the grain of prevalent norms and traditions, when people can break boundaries and criticize each other without hatred or malice; I am charmed by how we never lose a story, about how it reappears in a different form, how people are brought together, not by which god they believe in, but by the stories that they know and share; I am fascinated by how social realities leak into the plays, how the plays are influenced by ideas and behaviours around themselves, how they speak to and from the historical moment in which they were written.

But there is also much in the plays that makes me uncomfortable. Those are the very things that I must be clear-eyed about, for the plays are also ways of knowing the past and understanding the present. The multivalence of a polyglot universe excites me. I feel uplifted by the idea that people can speak many languages, but there is no joy in knowing that access to languages and the universes of meaning they contain was restricted by caste and gender. I think about how women are depicted, how the most basic agency over one's self and one's choices seems to be restricted to courtesans and nuns, women who have opted out of patriarchal structures.

There are also instances of caste stereotyping: the hero/king always has a brahmin companion, the vidushaka, who is usually comedic – a parody without malice of a brahmin who is everything the (usually kshatriya) hero is not. The brahmin is always hungry, greedy for food and money, cowardly, lazy and overweight. Plays as different in tone and intent as 'Shakuntala' and 'Nagananda' include this brahmin companion to the hero, but to my mind, the best examples of the vidushaka in this selection of plays are Maitreya in 'The Little Clay Cart' and Vasantaka in 'Malavika and Agnimitra' – lazy and avaricious, yes, but also loyal, quick thinking and very funny, using their wit to alert us to the vanities and foibles of their friends. In short, perfect dramatic foils to the protagonists. However, in Nagananda, when Atreya, the brahmin, is being teased by a drunk retainer and his lady friend, he is not amused when they suggest that he drink from the cup that the woman has already drunk from so that he can savour the sweetness of her lips as well as the wine, or when they mock him for having lost his sacred thread, a marker of his caste. Atreya announces that he is not amused and immediately goes off to purify himself of their touch and proximity.

Social hierarchy and caste are also visible in Sanskrit plays when women and minor characters, especially those who serve, speak in various Prakrits. Access to Sanskrit was already a feature of caste and gender in the first millennium, and it would be worthwhile for us to acknowledge all the aspects of social reality that are being referenced in Sanskrit plays by these linguistic shifts. These alternating registers and languages do not disturb the dramatic movement of the play: one assumes that the high caste characters, almost always men, can understand Prakrit, even if they do not deign to speak it. But we are left in an odd limbo of suspended disbelief – do the women understand what their lovers or masters or other men are saying to them?

In the plays in this volume, there are two kinds of women who can and do, sometimes, speak Sanskrit: the courtesan Vasantasena in 'The Little Clay Cart' and the Buddhist nun Kamandaki, in 'Malati and Madhava'. One way to think about women who can and do speak Sanskrit is this – nuns and courtesans are both 'outsiders', free from gendered norms and conventions because of their relationship with their bodies. The courtesan celebrates her body while the nun denies it. Whether these bodies are defined by indulgence (as with the courtesan) or by austerity (for the nun), they are fundamentally subversive in a universe where the female body's primary importance comes from various conjugal obligations, including procreation. The courtesan and the nun effectively function as casteless because their bodies are beyond the reach of patriarchal control, which also gives them more and greater freedoms and privileges even though they are women.

Speculations and questions like these point to the larger issue of how we might read literature from the past in general. Like all literatures from all cultures and all times, our literary works too, read and write the world of their creation for us. For that reason, they are necessary complements to historical information, telling us what monuments, geographies and inscriptions will not. How then, do we receive and evaluate what world literatures show us? In this case, we cannot deny what the plays are telling us about caste and gender, and we cannot fail to notice that they are exclusively about the adventures and amusements of social elites. It is only 'The Little Clay Cart' that acknowledges the existence of an urban proletariat and allows their aspirations to enter the play, indeed, to bring the play to its climax. That could well account for its continued popularity and multiple adaptations in contemporary Indian theatre.

Literatures animate the human silences that often surround material history. In doing so, they can provide parallel or alternative narratives about the past. Rather than see these alternatives as false or malicious because they make us uncomfortable, we need to include them in our world views so as to expand our ideas about who we are now and how we came to be this way. To have a single narrative of the past that we hold to be the truth is as misleading as it is, ultimately, dangerous. Both beauty and cruelty are a part of human experience, it would behoove us to acknowledge and understand both. The plays in this volume, I believe, can contribute to that more complete understanding.

MALAVIKA AND AGNIMITRA

BY KALIDASA

The plot of *Malavikagnimitram,* a story about a king's infatuation with a young woman who is part of his wife's palace retinue, probably has a historical source. Kalidasa foregrounds the love story, which is filled with overheard conversations, plots and intrigues, lies, betrayals and mistaken identities. The prime mover behind these is the king's friend, Gautama, the *vidushaka,* beloved by audiences and playwrights alike. This comic character is lazy, a glutton for food and luxury, and cowardly but with a cheerful, scheming intelligence that he uses to further his patron's ends. This comedy of errors plays out against the backdrop of a distant war for territory, where Agnimitra's generals and ministers are using force as well as diplomacy to subdue a neighbouring kingdom. It's likely that Kalidasa's historical source for this – the expansion of the Sunga Empire at the turn of the millennium under its second monarch, Agnimitra. Having chosen this real event as the context for his love story, Kalidasa exploits its potential to enhance the plot of his play, using a faraway political disturbance as the reason for a young woman to enter the palace of an ally incognito. Unlike 'Shakuntala', this play is led by the temperaments and desires of its female characters.

List of Important Characters

Agnimitra – king of Vidisha
Bakula – young woman in Queen Dharini's retinue
Dharini – Agnimitra's Chief Queen
Gautama – Agnimitra's companion and close friend
Ganadasa and Haradatta – dance teachers
Iravati – Agnimitra's Junior Queen
Kaumudika – young woman in Queen Dharini's retinue
Kaushiki – Buddhist nun and Queen Dharini's confidante
Malavika – new addition to Queen Dharini's retinue

Two young maids who looked after Queen Dharini bumped into each other as they went about their tasks for the day. Bakula was on her way to see the dance teacher employed by the royal court to check on the progress of his student Malavika, another young woman in the queen's retinue. Kaumudika was carrying a beautiful new ring in the shape of a snake that the queen's jeweller had just made. The maids admired the ring together as its gem stones caught the light. 'Has the king seen Malavika, even though she has been kept away from his sight?' asked Kaumudika. 'Oh yes,' giggled Bakula. 'He saw a picture of her in the gallery. He was passing by and saw the queen looking at a new painting of herself and all her attendants. The king stopped to talk to her and he noticed a lovely young woman in the painting. He asked repeatedly who she was, but the queen ignored his questions. But then, the little princess told her father that the girl in the painting was Malavika!' 'Such innocence!' laughed Kaumudika. 'You can be sure that Malavika was immediately sent into the depths of the palace, to rooms where the king would never run into her, not even by accident!' cried Bakula. 'I must go now,' said Kaumudika. 'The queen is waiting to see her new ring.'

Bakula found the dance teacher. 'Sir,' she said. 'The queen has sent me to find out about Malavika's progress in your class. Is she giving you trouble?' 'Not at all, not at all, it's quite the opposite,' said the teacher enthusiastically. 'She is so talented, so intelligent, so quick to learn! Where did the queen find her, this rare and wonderful creature?' Bakula told the teacher that Malavika had been sent to the queen by her brother who was posted at the border of the kingdom. He asked the queen to employ the girl he had sent as a gift in the palace in some artistic pursuits. 'Ah, she is a gift to me, too, this girl,' sighed the teacher as he continued on his way.

King Agnimitra was with his ministers, inquiring about the affairs of the kingdom and the safety of his borders. 'What's happening in Vidarbha?' asked the king. 'The king of Vidarbha has sent a reply to your letter in which you demanded the release of Madhavasena, who is soon to be your son-in-law, and his family,' said the minister. 'He says in his letter: "Your Majesty should know how to conduct himself when dealing with someone of equal stature. Madhavasena's sister is missing, but we are making efforts to find her. If you want Madhavasena released, then give up Mauryasachiva, my brother-in-law!"'

'Nonsense!' shouted the king. 'Does this fool really think he's my equal? Order General Virasena to implement the plan – it's time to get rid of this idiot who dares to challenge me!' 'A good idea, My Lord,' said the minister. 'He has just ascended to the throne, and this is a good time to remove him before he wins the hearts of his people.'

As the king was about to depart from his court, his friend Gautama entered. The king had previously asked Gautama to set up a secret meeting for him with Malavika, the treasured object of his recent attentions. Gautama whispered in the king's ear. 'Well done, friend, well done!' said the king, clearly very pleased with whatever Gautama had said to him. At that very moment, loud voices were heard from another room. The king's chamberlain came rushing in. 'Sire, the two dance teachers, Ganadasa and Haradatta, they wish to see you most urgently!' 'Send them in,' said the king as he sat down again. The dance teachers stumbled into the court, praising the king and his many virtues. The king called for seats for them and when they seemed more composed, he asked why they wanted to see him. Greatly agitated, interrupting one another and speaking incoherently, the teachers began to tell the king how each had insulted the other and how each was superior to the other as a teacher. They asked the king to be the judge of which of them was truly the better. The king was amused: this was a fine distraction from the important affairs of state that he had been dealing with. He said that Queen Dharini should also be a part of so major a decision, and so he summoned his wife and her friend, the nun Kaushiki.

The king welcomed his wife with affection and the nun with all the honours that were due to her. 'Take this seat,' he said to Kaushiki. 'These esteemed teachers are squabbling over who is superior. The queen and I have our favourites, but you, good lady, are truly learned and impartial. You should be the one to resolve this dispute.' Kaushiki replied, 'We know that they are both excellent dancers themselves, but the dispute is about who is the better teacher, is it not? In that case, we need to see their pupils, how they dance, how well the teacher has imparted his skills.' 'Right! Right!' shouted Gautama. 'That's the way for us to know who is better!' Ganadasa and Haradatta were both pleased with the plan, but the queen seemed displeased. 'That's not fair. What if the student is too stupid, or too untalented, or too new to fully absorb all she has been taught?' 'Surely that, too, would be the teacher's fault, for picking a poor student,' said the king. 'Your pupil is so new, Ganadasa,' said the queen quietly. 'How could she possibly have enough experience to perform in a competition?' Kaushiki chose a dance piece that both teachers had prepared with their students, and the king graciously led the queen to where they could sit comfortably and enjoy the performance. 'If only you were as clever in matters of the state,' thought the queen as she noticed the king's eagerness.

Because Ganadasa was older, he was given the honour of having his pupil perform first. The king said softly to Gautama, 'I can't wait to see that girl again!' 'Here she comes, My Lord,' Gautama whispered back. 'She is even lovelier than in the painting!' thought the king. 'I was sure that the painter had exaggerated her beauty, but the truth is, in fact, the opposite.' Ganadasa's student was Malavika and she sang a song of unrequited love, begging her beloved to come to her. 'She's singing to you, My Lord,' said Gautama. 'I know,' replied the king. 'How else could she declare her love for me in front of the queen? She has hidden her love in this song!' Malavika turned to leave the stage when she had finished, but Gautama stopped her. 'Wait, child! You haven't heard our comments on your performance.' The king almost swooned with love, noticing all her perfections as she stood before him.

Ganadasa invited Kaushiki to say what she thought. Kaushiki was full of praise for the young dancer, and Ganadasa beamed with satisfaction. But Gautama said, 'You failed in one aspect, good teacher. This is her first performance and you did not give a gift to a brahmin of good standing!' 'Sire, this is not her first performance,' said Ganadasa. 'Never mind, let me compliment the young lady with a suitable gift anyway,' said Gautama, unruffled. He slipped a bracelet off the king's arm and offered it to Malavika. 'But wait,' said the queen. 'How can you give her a prize when you haven't even seen the other dancer?' Ganadasa led Malavika away, and Gautama whispered to the king, 'This is as much as I can do for you.' The king looked downcast as Malavika left the stage. Haradatta bustled in, praising the king and announcing his student's performance. At that very moment, the town crier called midday. 'My goodness,' Gautama cried out. 'It is time for the brahmins to be fed. And your meal will be served immediately after that. Do not delay, Your Majesty, your doctors have advised a strict routine for your meals. Haradatta, can your student perform tomorrow?' A disappointed Haradatta had no choice but to surrender to the king's schedule, and the king and Gautama found themselves alone. 'My heart has been pierced by the arrows of love,' moaned the king. 'Make a plan for me to see Malavika again. I shall remain sleepless until then.'

Soon, all the palace maids were agog with the news that Malavika had won the dance contest and with rumours about the king and Malavika, and their undeclared love for each other. The morose king wandered through the palace in Gautama's company. He had grown thin and pale, pining for his new love. 'All these tears and sighs do not become you, My Lord,' said Gautama. 'I have sent Malavika your message through Bakula, but the queen guards Malavika as closely as the cobra guards the gem in his hood. Come, let us go into the pleasure garden. It is springtime: trees and bushes are in flower, the birds sing sweetly, and the breeze is laden with fragrances from the forest.'

The two men strolled into the garden, enjoying the alternating sunshine and shade, and went towards the grove where an ashoka tree grew. Malavika entered the grove, looking around distractedly. 'What is the point of being in love with a man who does not love me?' she sighed. 'How can I explain this to my friends? How long will the God of Love torment me like this?' She took a few steps and stopped. 'Where am I?' she said. 'Ah, I remember. The queen told me to stand in for her in the ritual to make the ashoka tree bloom. She would have done it herself, but she has injured her foot because of that careless man, Gautama. I am to touch the tree with my left foot, and if it flowers within five days, the queen will give me a gift, something that will make my wish come true. I seem to be in the right grove, but I'll wait for Bakula to bring me the ornaments for my feet.'

Gautama, walking ahead of the king, saw Malavika sitting sadly by herself. He alerted the king, who could not believe his luck. 'She is even more beautiful in her sadness,' he said as he gazed at the young woman, who wore her hair in a single braid and no ornaments at all. The king and Gautama hid themselves and watched the young woman as she sighed and spoke aloud to herself about her heartache. Bakula slipped into the ashoka grove, her hands filled with ornaments for Malavika's feet to prepare for her ritual at the ashoka tree. She took Malavika's feet into her lap and began to decorate them with red lac and adorn them with Queen Dharini's precious anklets. In the bushes, the king sighed deeply as he gazed upon the perfection of his beloved's foot.

Iravati, the junior queen, had also wandered into the area around the grove with her maid. She had been drinking and was a little unsteady on her feet. She was surprised to see Malavika being prepared for the ashoka tree ceremony. 'Why is she getting this honour?' she said peevishly to her maid but she was persuaded to stay silent and say no more. Bakula had finished decorating

Malavika's foot with delicate streaks of lac and was admiring her handiwork. Overcome by the beauty of the foot, she said, 'Dear Malavika, may you always be by the king's side! I know he has feelings for you, I heard him say so. Be patient. All will be well.' In her hiding place, Queen Iravati's maid gasped, 'Oh, the cheek of this serving girl, how dare she!' 'But I am so afraid of Queen Dharini!' cried Malavika. 'Promise me that you will always be my friend, whatever happens!' Bakula comforted Malavika and urged her to touch the ashoka tree which was now covered with auspicious designs and adorned with Queen Dharini's own anklet. 'Do as the queen commanded,' she said. 'Let the ashoka bloom!'

The king could wait no longer. 'Gautama,' he pleaded. 'Please, let us reveal ourselves!' 'I shall tease this young woman and make her blush,' declared his friend. He stepped out from behind the bushes. 'Oho! What is this I see? You have kicked the sacred ashoka tree? Bakula, you should know better! Why did you let her act so inappropriately?' The two young women cried out, 'It's the king, it's the king!' Iravati and her maid, who were still hidden, were equally surprised to see the king. Bakula spoke quickly: 'Sire, please, she is only obeying Queen Dharini's instructions. You must forgive her!' She threw herself at the king's feet, and Malavika did the same.

The king raised Malavika up and said, 'There is nothing to fear. You have not committed any error. But look! Your delicate foot is not injured, even though it touched the rough bark of the tree!' Malavika blushed and said, 'Let us return to the queen and tell her that we have done as she commanded.' Bakula said, 'The king must excuse us before we can leave his presence.' 'I have one condition,' said the king. 'Like this tree, I, too, have been unfulfilled this season. I, too, long for a loving touch . . . ' 'I am sure you do!'

said Iravati loudly as she entered the grove. 'Go on, Malavika, attend to your king's wishes!' 'Run!' whispered Gautama to the king. 'Or, say something quickly, say something to save your skin!' 'Dear Iravati, I was just amusing myself while I waited for you. Come, now,' cajoled the king. 'I'm sure that's true,' retorted Iravati. 'I'm only sorry I interrupted your game!' 'Our king is known for being courteous,' said Gautama, trying to pour oil on troubled waters. 'How can you be angry with him for his natural good manners when he makes small talk with his wife's maid?' 'Small talk, was it?' snorted Iravati. 'Well then, I should hardly pay it any attention.' She lifted the hem of her skirt as she flounced off, but she tripped over its hem.

The king went after her, begging her forgiveness. 'Go away, you unfaithful man!' she cried as she stumbled on. 'Unfaithful! Such harsh words for me!' said the king. 'Look, your girdle has fallen and clings to me, as you should!' Iravati tried to take the girdle from him, but the king took this opportunity to fall at her feet. 'Get up!' said Iravati, irritated with the king's antics. 'These are not Malavika's feet, that would make you feel fulfilled!' She left the grove, seething with anger.

Some days later, the king sent Gautama to bring news of Malavika. But what Gautama had to tell him was not pleasant at all. Queen Dharini had heard from Iravati about the episode by the ashoka tree and had imprisoned both Malavika and Bakula in an underground chamber. Their guard had been told that no one could see them unless they carried the queen's own signet ring. The king was terribly dejected when he heard this, but Gautama said that he had a plan, and when he whispered in the king's ear, the king began to smile. He called for Jayasena, the doorkeeper, and told Gautama to share the plan with him. Then, taking Jayasena with him, the king went to call on the queen, who was listening to Kaushiki's stories in the Room of the Breezes.

The king inquired about Dharini's injured foot with great affection, and she replied that she was, indeed, better. Just then, Gautama rushed in, heaving and panting and in a state of great agitation. He flung himself to the floor, throwing his limbs about as he moaned and groaned. 'Save me, Majesty, save me! I was bitten by a snake, a cobra, no less, when I was gathering blossoms from the ashoka tree for the queen! Save me, I beg you!' Kaushiki began to suggest that the usual remedy was to remove the poison . . . but the king interrupted and shouted to Jayasena to send for the poison master immediately. 'I am dying!' moaned Gautama. 'Sire, we have been companions since our childhood. Promise me you will look after my wife and children when I am dead!'

Jayasena came back with the message that the doctor had asked for Gautama to be brought to him without delay and that he was preparing to perform the water pot ritual for the afflicted man. For that, he would need an object decorated with the image of a snake. 'Take my ring,' said Queen Dharini quickly. 'It is marked with a snake. Return it to me as soon as the doctor has finished with it.' Another courtier came in and said that the king's ministers were waiting for him to discuss matters of state, and as the king left to join them, he suggested that his wife be taken to the inner chambers of the palace.

Instead of heading to his courtroom, the king hurried off to meet Gautama, who had executed the second part of his plan by then. 'What happened?' asked the king as soon as he saw Gautama. 'Did the guard believe you? What did you say?' Gautama replied,

'How could she refuse a messenger who carried the queen's signet ring? She had to release those poor girls. But to make it more urgent, I said that the royal astrologer had said that the king was going through a phase of bad luck and that he advised the king to pardon and release all his prisoners. But come, now! We must go quickly to where Malavika is waiting for you!'

Gautama had left Malavika and Bakula in a little house near a pond, and the two men made their way there. 'I wonder what my beloved does when she's waiting for me,' mused the king. 'Let's watch through the window.' They crept to the side of the house and listened to the young women talking. 'Greet the king, Malavika. Honour him with praise,' said Bakula. 'Where, where is he?' cried Malavika as she spun around in confusion. 'Oh, you are mean! This is just his portrait,' she said disappointed. 'But who is he looking at so lovingly?' 'That's Iravati,' replied Bakula. 'It's not very nice of him to look at only one of his women like that,' said Malavika. 'Iravati is the king's favourite,' said Bakula feeling mischievous. 'Oh, why then am I making myself so miserable with my love for him?' sighed Malavika.

The king decided that it was time to show himself. 'Lady, ignore the picture. Here I am, before you now, with only you in my heart!' Gautama and Bakula made an excuse to leave, but the king told them to keep watch and ensure that no other people came by. Gautama lay down on a crystal bench in the shade of a tree, and in minutes, he was fast asleep.

'Why are you so afraid of me?' the king asked Malavika gently. 'You should cling to me as a jasmine vine clings to a mango tree!' 'I am afraid of the queen,' said Malavika. The king tried to take Malavika in his arms, but she moved away. Meanwhile, Iravati and her maid, who were looking for Gautama, ran into Queen Dharini's attendant. She told them that the queen was no longer angry and that she had set free the two women Iravati had complained to her about. Iravati sent a message back saying she was grateful to be in the queen's favour again.

Iravati and her maid found Gautama asleep in the shade, mumbling in his sleep. They crept closer to hear what he was saying. Iravati flew into a rage when she realized that Gautama was babbling about how beautiful Malavika was and how she was the king's favourite. Her maid picked up the twisted branch of a tree that looked like a snake and threw it at Gautama. 'That'll teach this snake-fearing fellow a lesson!' she said. Gautama jumped up shouting, 'A snake! A snake! Help, help!' In a second, the king was by his friend's side, reassuring him. Iravati rushed to him. 'I see that you enjoy your flirtations in the broad daylight,' she said angrily.

The king was surprised to see Iravati and quickly tried to pretend that he was happy to have run into her. He tried to calm her down with sweet words: that she had no reason to be angry with him, that she was still his favourite, and that he had had the two women released from prison only because the festival was a day of happy celebration. But Iravati's maid arrived from Queen Dharini's chambers and whispered something in her mistress's ear. Iravati turned on Gautama. 'Your plot is unravelling, you cunning man!' she said. Gautama was saved from further abuse by a doorkeeper who ran in shouting, 'Our little princess, she has been frightened by a monkey. She is with the queen now. She is very agitated and will not calm down!' Iravati cried, 'Go to her, My Lord, she needs you!' In his heart, Gautama blessed the monkey and wiped the sweat from his brow. He hurried out with the king.

The woman who looked after the ashoka grove came into the garden saying, 'Malavika is so lucky! Look! The ashoka tree has flowered and the queen has given up her anger. But what is this hunchback Sarasaka doing here, I wonder? And why is he carrying a jewel? I shall ask him.' Sarasaka said, 'I'm taking this to the royal priest as payment for the ritual the queen requested when she learned that her son was to guard the sacrificial horse. She wants the gods to protect him. She is in the temple now, listening to the good news that her brother, Virasena, has captured the king of Vidarbha and that Madhavasena, our ally, has been set free. Madhavasena has sent the king many gifts – horses and gold coins and jewels.' The grove-keeper thanked the hunchback for the news and made her way to the queen's chambers.

Shouts of praise for the king filled the air. Gautama said, 'I heard the queen say to Kaushiki that she should dress Malavika in bridal splendour. I think she intends to make you happy.' 'Dharini always has my happiness at heart – once she gets over her rage!' said the king. A doorkeeper announced that the queen wanted to enjoy the pleasure of viewing the flowering ashoka tree in the king's company and that she was making her way to the grove at that very moment with her retinue of attendants, including Malavika.

Queen Dharini greeted the king with all courtesy when he entered the grove and pointed out the beauty of the flowering tree. The royal chamberlain joined them with news about the victory over Vidarbha. 'Among the gifts from Vidarbha are these two girls, skilled in all the arts. They are now ready for an audience with you.' He summoned the girls and presented them to the king. The girls honoured the king and received his greetings. 'What arts are you skilled in, my dears?' he asked. 'We can sing,' they said, and the king offered one of them to Dharini. The queen called Malavika and asked which of the girls she would like as a companion. The moment the girls saw Malavika, they fell to their knees, whispering to each other, 'This is our king's daughter!' 'What is this?' said the king. 'Who are you? Who is she?' 'Your forces released Prince Madhavasena from captivity. This is his sister!' 'Oh no! I imprisoned a woman of royal birth!' cried Queen Dharini. 'But how did she get here?' said the king, his confusion increasing. One of the girls said, 'When the prince was imprisoned by his wicked kinsman, his loyal minister, Sumati, quickly sent away the prince's sister.' 'Yes, yes, we know that part,' said the king impatiently. 'Then what happened?'

Kaushiki stepped forward. 'Let me tell you the rest,' she said quietly. The girls said to each other, 'Can that be Kaushiki? We didn't recognize her, dressed as a nun!' Gautama broke in, 'Will someone tell us the rest of the story, please!' Kaushiki said, 'I am the sister of Sumati, the minister. When Madhavasena was captured, Sumati fled with Malavika and me, and hoping to reach you, he joined a caravan of merchants. But when we entered a forest, we were attacked by a band of thieves and the soldiers who accompanied the caravan vanished. Sumati was killed while he was trying to protect Malavika. I fainted with grief, and when I came back to consciousness, Malavika was nowhere to be found. I only saw her again when we both became part of the queen's retinue. I learned that Malavika had been rescued by forest dwellers and handed over to the queen.' 'But why didn't you tell us who she was?' spluttered the queen. 'I had a reason, My Lady,' said Kaushiki. 'A fortune teller said, long ago, that Malavika would make a very good marriage only after she had lived for a year as a serving girl. I decided to help this wonderful prophecy come true, so I kept silent.'

'All's well that ends well,' said the king relieved. 'And we have just received news that our son, who was protecting the sacrificial horse, has been victorious against an army that challenged him.' The queen was delighted and, in her happiness, she sent one of her maids to the inner chambers to tell Iravati that she should forget all that had happened and embrace Malavika as a friend rather than treat her as a rival for the king's affections. She said to Kaushiki, 'As the minister Sumati had intended, I will now ask King Agnimitra to take Malavika as a wife.' 'Dear Dharini,' said Agnimitra. 'I knew you had my welfare at heart. May you always love me and may I always live under your generous gaze!'

NAGANANDA

BY HARSHA

The playwright Harsha is thought to be none other than Harshavardhana (590–647 CE), who ruled from Kannauj in northern India. Like many other Hindu rulers of his time, Harshavardhana was open-minded and generous towards other religions. He allowed their free and unencumbered practice as well as built and supported their places of worship and religious institutions. Xuanxang, the Chinese scholar-pilgrim who visited Harsha's court, stated in no uncertain terms that the emperor was a devout Buddhist, although other historical records have described his family as worshippers of Surya and the king himself as a Shaivite.

Whoever he might have been and whatever his own religious beliefs, Harsha the playwright has given us a play that lives and breathes outside conventional Hindu values and behaviours. The source is the *Brihatkatha,* itself a compendium of stories that inhabit a pluralist and diverse universe of religious practices and beliefs. In *Nagananda,* Harsha explores the life and deeds of the bodhisattva Jimutavahana, who waits for the opportunity to sacrifice his life for the good of others. The first half of the play walks the familiar path of a prince who falls in love with a woman he does not know and, with the help of various friends and companions, finally wins her love. But the second half of the play veers off into a territory that could not be further from the classical dramatic trope of lovers who are temporarily separated and suffer heartbreak but are destined to reunite in a happy ending.

List of Important Characters

Atreya – Jimutavahana's friend
Chaturika – Malayavati's companion
Garuda – king of the birds
Jimutavahana – vidyadhara prince, in love with Malayavati
Malayavati – princess who marries Jimutavahana
Mitravasu – Malayavati's brother
Navamalika – serving girl in the palace, beloved of Shekharaka
Shankhachuda – young Naga who is chosen as the sacrifice to Garuda
Shekharaka – lover of Navamalika
Vasuki – king of the Nagas

Jimutavahana was a vidyadhara prince, beloved of all and deeply devoted to his parents, whose comfort and welfare were foremost in his heart. 'Youth is a time of great passions, but it is fleeting and cannot be taken too seriously. I have decided to spend this time in my life looking after my aged parents who have retired to the forest to live simply, like ascetics,' Jimutavahana said to his friend Atreya. Atreya disagreed: 'Come now, you should enjoy the pleasures of kingship while you are young. I can see that you have had enough of this caring and I'm not surprised.' 'Surely those pleasures cannot outweigh the joy of serving one's parents. I really don't see what is so attractive about kingship, I see it as a burden,' replied Jimutavahana. Atreya was losing patience with his friend. 'It's not only pleasure that prompts me to talk to you about returning to the duties of kingship,' he said. 'What more can I do? My people are happy, my kingdom is peaceful and prosperous, I know that I have fulfilled all my duties in that regard.' Atreya tried another line of argument. 'Your enemy, Matanga, is far from quiet. I fear that in your absence he will try to usurp your position.' 'Let him,' said Jimutavahana simply. 'If it were up to me, I would have given him the kingdom. But my father would never agree to that. I think it's better that we occupy ourselves with my father's recent predicament. He told me that the place where they live is depleted. Firewood as well as food from plants, their roots and fruits and wild grains – all have been used up. He wants me to find them another suitable location on the Malaya mountain. Let us make a trip there.'

The two men set off to scout for a place with abundant water and edible plants, where the old king and queen could live with ease. As they climbed the mountain slopes, they were struck by its peaceful beauty – the weather was cool, the animals were calm, the plants and trees swaying in a gentle breeze were lush and green. They came upon a settlement of ascetics where the air was even sweeter, filled with bird songs and the chanting of sacred verses. 'What a lovely place,' Jimutavahana exclaimed. 'I think my parents would be happy living here.' 'I can hear someone singing,' Atreya said. 'Listen.' 'It seems to be coming from that temple. It must be some goddess who has come to earth. Let's go closer, but not enter, in case we are not worthy. We can listen from outside. Let's get behind this flowering bush.' From their hiding place, they could see a young woman playing a stringed instrument and singing to the goddess in the sweetest of voices. Atreya could barely contain his happiness when he saw that Jimutavahana was smitten by the young woman and could not take his eyes off her.

'This goddess that you worship and appease every day gives you nothing!' The young woman's attendant teased her with a smile. 'Ah, you are wrong!' the young woman, whose name was Malayavati, replied spiritedly. 'Just last night, she promised me in a dream that I would soon marry a vidyadhara prince!' 'We must seize this opportunity!' whispered Atreya. He grabbed his friend by the hand and pulled him out from behind the bush. 'Your dream has come true, young lady!' he said triumphantly. 'Who is this?' Malayavati whispered to her companion, for she was quite captivated by the stranger. 'Madam, I believe he is the man of your dreams!' her companion replied, echoing Atreya. 'I cannot stay here,' said Malayavati and turned away.

'My Lady, how is it that you do not honour a guest that has come to your home?' said Atreya boldly. Malayavati's companion, Chaturika by name and by nature, swiftly agreed, saying, 'It would be unseemly, madam, if you were not to welcome these gentlemen appropriately. I can do that on your behalf.' She turned to the visitors: 'Please be seated. Your good looks and noble carriage only enhance the beauty of this pleasant spot.'

King Vishvavasu, Malayavati's father, had learned that Jimutavahana, the vidyadhara prince, had come to the Malaya mountain and he quickly sent his son to meet him with an offer of marriage for his daughter. He also sent someone to look for Malayavati and bring her back to the settlement in time for the midday rituals. The ascetic in search of Malayavati entered the temple grove and could not help but notice the visitors. One, in particular, was strikingly handsome, his posture naturally regal and serene, and he seemed to carry all the auspicious marks on his person. The ascetic was sure that this was Jimutavahana himself, the future emperor of the vidyadharas. His heart overflowed with happiness when he saw how well-suited the young man and Malayavati were for each other and he smiled that destiny had already brought them together. 'Welcome, Your Majesty!' he said brightly. 'Oh, please do not rise. It is we who have to bow in your presence,' Malayavati said sweetly, acknowledging the nobility and sophistication of her guests. 'Now come with me, child,' the ascetic said to her.' Our spiritual father has sent for you so that we can start the midday rituals.' 'I would so much rather stay here, in the company of our honourable guest,' Malayavati thought to herself, but she knew she could not delay. And so she left but with many a sigh and backward glance at the handsome man who had stolen her heart. Jimutavahana, too, was sad to see her go.

A few days later, Malayavati told her attendants to prepare a cool bench of moonstone for her in the sandalwood grove, for her body had become heavy with the heat and weary from plucking flowers. The girls giggled among themselves as they prepared a cool seat for her, as they knew exactly what it was that was making her lethargic and dreamy. Even when they brought her there, Malayavati seemed absent-minded and charmingly distracted. She spoke her thoughts out loud, scolding the God of Love for tormenting her while he left the object of her affections alone. She sighed and said fretfully, 'This bower is completely shaded from the sun but I am still hot and feverish!' 'I can tell you why,' said Chaturika smiling. 'It's that man, he's made a home for himself in your heart. You cannot be happy unless you are with him. But don't you worry. I am sure he is as agitated as you are.' Chaturika anointed the princess with sandalwood juice and fanned her with large leaves, but Malayavati complained that these attentions made it all the more hotter. 'Is there a cure for this fever?' she asked. 'There certainly is,' Chaturika laughed. Aside, she whispered, 'If only he would come!'

In another part of the lush forest, Jimutavahana was suffering in a similar way. 'The God of Love has struck me with flower arrows even though I am already so deeply wounded by the glances of that dark-eyed girl!' he cried. 'You tell me that I am no longer firm and steadfast even when I have endured these scented breezes, these moonlit nights, the sweet songs of birds. But you are right: I am no longer strong since even arrows made of flowers cause me pain!' Atreya felt sorry for his friend. 'Tell me, why have you left your parents alone and come here again so soon?' 'I dreamt last night that my beloved sat somewhere here in a sandalwood grove. She was in tears as if I had hurt her in some way. I want to find that grove with the moonstone bench so that I can lie there and feel her presence,' said the forlorn vidyadhara prince.

Malayavati and her companion ran to hide when they heard footsteps approaching the grove. Chaturika could not conceal her excitement when she saw who it was. Jimutavahana flung himself onto the moonstone bench and recalled his dream aloud, the one in which he was unable to soothe his distressed beloved. 'I wonder who he is talking about,' Malayavati said as her heart began to beat faster. 'It has to be you, My Lady,' said Chaturika. 'It can be no one else!' 'Let's wait to hear the end of this conversation so that we can find out more,' Malayavati said, too nervous to take Chaturika seriously. They heard Jimutavahana ask Atreya to fetch him some red arsenic so that he could draw his beloved's face on the bench. When he had completed the portrait, Jimutavahana said, 'I feel as if I'm in her presence. This portrait is like a balm on my aching heart.' In her hiding place, Malayavati shuddered. 'I cannot bear to hear any more. Let us go and find my brother Mitravasu, he must be back by now.'

Malayavati's father told Mitravasu that since they had now seen Jimutavahana at close quarters, it was clear that he was, indeed, the most suitable groom for Malayavati and that Mitravasu should go ahead and formalise the alliance. Mitravasu was pleased with what he had seen of Jimutavahana – his good looks, his pleasing demeanour, his modesty and his courage. 'But I don't like the fact that his compassionate nature makes him ready to give up his life for any living creature,' he said to himself. 'Anyway, I've heard he is here, in this sandalwood grove. I shall go and meet him.'

Atreya was very excited to see Mitravasu, for he knew who he was. 'Quickly, friend,' he said to Jimutavahana. 'Cover up the portrait that you have drawn, we don't want the siddha prince to see it.' The princes greeted each other warmly and asked after each other's families. 'I have a message for you from my father,' said Mitravasu. 'He says, "I have a lovely daughter of marriageable age, I offer her to you as a bride." Hidden among the bushes outside the grove, the two girls listened eagerly to this conversation. They heard Jimutavahana say quietly to Atreya. 'It looks like I have a problem.' 'Yes, I can see,' Atreya agreed. 'With your mind set on that girl, you cannot even think of another. Send him away with some polite refusal.' 'Oh, this can only mean one thing,' whispered Malayavati. 'I am honoured by your proposal,' said Jimutavahana carefully. 'But a mind set in one direction cannot be turned around. I fear that I cannot accept your sister.' Malayavati fell to the ground in a faint. 'You know that he does not make decisions entirely by his own choice,' Atreya said to Mitravasu, trying to lessen the sting of Jimutavahana's rejection. 'Go and speak to his parents and ask for their permission.' 'I will do that, I will go and meet his father. The prince cannot refuse us after we have made this proposal so openly!' Mitravasu said and left, determined to persuade Jimutavahana's father to accept the marriage proposal.

'How can my brother even speak to this vile man who has insulted us so,' Malayavati thought, distraught. 'I have no need for this body anymore, it brings me only sorrow and suffering. I will hang myself right here with that beautiful creeper.' Chaturika ran to Jimutavahana and cried, 'Help, help! She's trying to hang herself from that ashoka tree!' Jimutavahana ran back to the grove. He took Malayavati's hand and untied the creeper she had placed around her neck. 'Let me go!' Malayavati said indignantly. 'You have no right to touch me!' 'This is all your friend's fault,' Chaturika said to Atreya. 'That portrait of a woman that he drew on the bench, My Lady took that to mean that he has some other beloved because he refused Mitravasu's proposal, which was for her hand in marriage!' 'Ah, this is she. This is Malayavati herself!' Jimutavahana's heart skipped a beat. 'If that is the case, my friend is innocent,' said Atreya, full of smiles. 'Go and take a look at that portrait.'

Malayavati shyly tried to pull her hand away, but she was blushing and smiling up at the prince through her eyelashes. 'I cannot let go of this sweet hand,' said Jimutavahana. 'Come and see my heart's desire drawn on that stone.' Malayavati was embarrassed when she saw the drawing that had been covered with a banana leaf. 'All's well, then,' said Atreya. 'Your commitment ceremony is now complete, you can let go of her hand.' An excited young woman came running into the grove. 'My Lady, you have been accepted by Jimutavahana's parents. Mitravasu has sent me here to say that you must come with me at once, your wedding ceremony has been fixed for today!' 'We need to prepare ourselves for this wedding, too!' said Jimutavahana, and they all left.

Soon after, a drunkard named Shekharaka was tottering around, accompanied by his servant. 'I am so fortunate. I have a woman to love, wine in my mouth and a servant who caters to all my needs,' he slurred. 'But, hey! What's this? Someone is pushing against me. Ah, it must be my beloved Navamalika!' 'She's not here, master,' said his servant. 'What do you mean?' asked Shekharaka. 'Malayavati's wedding ceremony is long concluded. Where can she be? I suppose everyone from the wedding party is drinking and carousing in the flower garden. Navamalika must be there, too. Let me go look for her.'

Atreya was also enjoying a stroll in the garden when, suddenly, he was attacked by a swarm of bees. He had dressed up as a woman for the wedding festivities and was able to protect himself by covering his head with the veil from his costume. Shekharaka bumped into him, and mistaking Atreya for his beloved Navamalika, he embraced him tightly and tried to stuff some betel nut into his mouth. Atreya recoiled from the smell of the wine and tried to wriggle out of Shekharaka's arms. Shekharaka fell at Atreya's feet crying, 'Navamalika, don't be angry, darling!' Just then, Navamalika came down the path, returning from the bower that had been decorated for the newlyweds. 'I'm done with that, good. Now, I can look for Shekharaka, who must be lusting for me since I was away last night,' she thought. 'Well, look at that! Here he is, flirting with some other woman!'

'Navamalika! I, who do not even bow to the gods, I touch your feet!' babbled Shekharaka. 'You idiot! There is no Navamalika here!' shouted Atreya. Navamalika, meanwhile, pretended to be angry and teased her lover by sulking, but Atreya had had enough of the drunken antics and revealed himself. 'You'd better do something to make up for harassing this poor man,' Navamalika said sternly to Shekharaka, who poured some more wine. 'Drink up, Navamalika! Then this fine gentleman can drink from the same cup and savour the sweetness of your lips as well as the wine!'

'I am a brahmin,' Atreya said disgusted. 'Really? Where is your sacred thread?' demanded Shekharaka. 'You ripped it off when I was struggling to get out of your embrace,' Atreya said sourly. 'Why don't you recite some sacred verses, then?' said Navamalika, who was feeling quite cheeky and joined in with Shekharaka's teasing. Atreya was no longer amused. 'Would you like me to lay my head at your feet?' he asked sarcastically. Navamalika realized that the mood of the encounter had changed. 'Please, please, do not be angry,' she begged. 'We were only joking!' 'I forgive you,' Atreya said, and went off to bathe in the tank as he had been polluted by his contact with the drunk Shekharaka.

Atreya saw Malayavati and Jimutavahana approaching, dressed in their wedding finery. They were accompanied by Chaturika, who was leading them to the bower that had been prepared for them. Jimutavahana could not take his eyes off his lovely bride and was whispering sweet nothings into her delicate shell-like ears. Atreya greeted them at the entrance and led them to a crystal seat, for Malayavati seemed tired after the walk. Chaturika and Atreya amused the couple with their jokes and banter for a little while, and then Mitravasu arrived to speak privately with Jimutavahana.

When they were alone, Mitravasu told Jimutavahana that his kingdom had been attacked by the wicked Matanga and that he, Mitravasu, was ready to kill that cowardly enemy in battle. Jimutavahana was upset by this talk of violence, and he said, 'You know that, out of compassion, I would give up my life for any other living being. I cannot permit this killing for the sake of a kingdom. For me, the only enemies are the three vices – ignorance, sensual attachments and hatred. Pity that poor fellow who has fallen victim to them! Come, the sun has set, let us go indoors!' But he knew that he had not been able to quell his brother-in-law's anger, and his heart was heavy.

Sometime later, Mitravasu and Jimutavahana were on the seashore, watching the play of the waves that were bright with the richly coloured gems they carried up from the ocean floor. Jimutavahana remarked on the beauty of the peaks of Malaya, shining white as if covered by autumn clouds. 'Those are not the peaks of Malaya,' Mitravasu corrected him. 'Those are heaps of Naga bones. This is where Garuda, king of the birds, used to eat one snake a day. He would part the waters and split the bottom of the ocean with the power of his wings, and then he would pull out a snake from the underworld and eat it. One day, Vasuki, king of the snakes, who feared that his entire race would perish, came to Garuda.' 'Did he say, "Eat me first?"' asked Jimutavahana. 'No,' Mitravasu continued with his story. 'Vasuki told Garuda that the female Nagas were anxious that their embryos were being born prematurely and were dying in thousands, a situation that was not to anyone's benefit, not even Garuda's. He offered to bring Garuda one snake a day to eat.' 'Just once, he could have said, "Here I am, in place of a snake" and saved a life,' Jimutavahana said. 'How easily people do bad things for the sake of this worthless body that is unclean, unreliable and will soon perish. I wish I could sacrifice my life to save even one Naga!'

A messenger arrived from the palace and said that the king had asked to see Mitravasu. The young prince went away with him, and Jimutavahana was left alone with his thoughts. Suddenly, he heard the sound of crying and turned around to see an old woman weeping as if her heart would break. She was accompanied by a young man, Shankhachuda. 'My son, my darling child, how can

I live through this day when you will be killed! Your beautiful young body, which has never seen the sun, will be devoured by Garuda!' 'Mother, why are you making it worse with all this wailing and crying? Mortality is the first nursemaid who clasps a baby to her breast, the mother is only the second. Let me go now!' Shankhachuda turned to the attendant who was with them and said, 'I am ready!'

The attendant took the young man to a rocky outcrop and dressed him in red garments. He spoke the message that Vasuki, the Naga king, had sent: 'You have put on the red garments so that Garuda can see and identify you easily. Climb to the top of the Rock of Execution so that the king of the birds can eat you!' Jimutavahana was watching from a distance with a growing sense of horror. He listened to the old woman crying and lamenting her son's fate and her own. The young man bravely tried to console her, but she was beyond comfort. 'How can I watch this?' Jimutavahana cried to himself and he stepped forward. The old woman threw herself at his feet. 'Eat me, take my body, great Garuda! Let my son live!' 'Mother, this is not Garuda,' said her son. 'Look at this wondrous being, he is so beautiful and so unlike Garuda, whose eyes are cruel and whose beak and claws are smeared with blood.' 'The whole world appears to me like Garuda today!' said the old woman. 'I will stand in for your son,' said Jimutavahana. 'Give me the clothes and the badge of the condemned man!' 'You, too, are a son to someone, and yet you wish to give up your body for the sake of my son who has been abandoned by his own people,' the old woman said, overcome.

Shankhachuda thought to himself, 'Who can this be, so willing to give up his life for me? How different he is from the rest of the world, treating his own life as a thing of no consequence.' He said to Jimutavahana, 'You have shown great compassion, but please, do not do this. Low-born people like me, our lives and deaths are unimportant, but people like you who live for the good of others, should remain alive!' 'I have waited so long for this opportunity to give myself up in the place of another, so please don't stand in my way,' said Jimutavahana. 'Think of something that will let my mother live beyond this day,' said Shankhachuda, determined to be the sacrificial victim. 'The only thing that will save her life is if you save yours,' said Jimutavahana, equally stubborn in his desire to sacrifice himself. 'How can you let your mother look upon that graveyard of the snakes, covered with bits of rotting flesh and slick with blood, surrounded by jackals and vultures? Come, give me that badge!' But Shankhachuda would not change his mind.

As the time of Garuda's daily arrival was approaching, Shankhachuda, along with his mother, decided to pay a last visit to a shrine that was close by. Again, Jimutavahana was alone. Unexpectedly, the king's chamberlain arrived with a rich suit of red clothing. 'The queen mother has sent this for you to wear on this auspicious day,' he said as he handed over the garments. 'This is most timely,' thought Jimutavahana. 'I will put on these red clothes and climb to the top of the execution rock where Garuda will see me clearly. I can sense that he is coming! Even memories of Malayavati do not give me as much pleasure as does the thought of what I am about to accomplish. Through all the merit I shall attain today, let me be born again in a body that I can sacrifice for others!' Garuda swooped down to the rock and picked up his prey. He carried him off to the top of Mount Malaya to eat at his leisure. Shankhachuda finished his visit to the shrine and came back to wait for Garuda. But he quickly realized that Jimutavahana had been taken in his place. He started to cry, praising the man who had saved him. Unwilling to live any more, he decided to follow the trail of blood that had been left on the forest floor when Garuda carried away his latest victim.

When Jimutavahana did not return for a long time, King Vishvavasu, grew concerned and sent one of his attendants to see if he was, perhaps, at his own home. The attendant went to Jimutavahana's father's dwelling to find the prince. There, he saw the old king, still radiant and majestic, sitting with his wife and daughter-in-law, but the prince was nowhere in sight. Jimutavahana's family became worried when they learned that he had not yet returned from his trip to the seashore. At that moment, a crest jewel covered in blood and gore fell into their midst. Jimutavahana's mother recognized it as her son's and burst into a flood of tears. The attendant reassured her that many such jewels fell in the area as they belonged to the Nagas that Garuda carried away. The family quickly sent the attendant back to Vishvavasu in the hope that Jimutavahana would have returned by the time he got there.

Jimutavahana's mother saw a man dressed in red coming towards them and was filled with dread. 'He looks so troubled, my lord,' she said to her husband. 'Let us ask him what is bothering him.' They stopped him and asked him who he was. Through his tears, Shankhachuda said, 'I am the Naga that was sent to appease Garuda's hunger. But a compassionate vidyadhara saved my life and gave himself up to the king of the birds.' The queen and Malayavati both fainted when they heard these words. 'This could only have been my son! Alas, what a terrible fate has befallen me!'

wailed the old king. He pressed the crest jewel to his breast, crying that this was all that he had left of his son. Both parents decided that they could not live without Jimutavahana and would burn themselves to death that very minute. Shankhachuda became more and more miserable, knowing, as he now did, that the entire family had been devastated by the loss of one man. He said, 'Let us not give up hope. Maybe when Garuda learns that the person he picked up was not a Naga, he will release him. I will follow the trail of blood to wherever Garuda is.' The old king said, 'You go on ahead. We will follow you after collecting some fire from the sacred altar.'

Shankhachuda set off. In the distance, he could see Garuda on the peak of Mount Malaya. Garuda was taken aback by the attitude of his latest victim. 'What kind of man is this?' he wondered. 'He does not seem at all agitated, his face is serene and he seems to feel nothing even though I have torn at his flesh. It is almost as if he is enjoying this. I'm not going to eat him. I want to know more about who he is.' 'Why have you stopped eating, Garuda?' said Jimutavahana. 'There is still flesh on my bones, and I know that your hunger is not yet satisfied.' 'Goodness, this fellow speaks so clearly, even in this state,' Garuda thought. He said, 'I want to know who you are.' At that moment, Shankhachuda arrived. 'Eat me, Garuda. I was the one sent today by Vasuki as your food. This man is not a Naga!' he shouted. 'But you are both wearing the red clothes that mark you as my food!' replied the bird. 'Look at me closely,' said Shankhachuda. 'Can you not see scales on my body, my forked tongue as I speak? See – here are my three hoods, and look how my gems are obscured by the fumes of my deadly venom! This is Jimutavahana, best among all the vidyadharas. You cannot eat him!'

Garuda realized that he had made a terrible mistake. 'This is the Jimutavahana that I have heard about – people everywhere praise him, bards from the highest mountains to the lowest plains sing of him. He volunteered his own body in place of the Naga. I have committed the ghastly sin of eating a bodhisattva. There is no expiation for this other than burning myself to death. Oh, look! Some people are walking towards us, and they are carrying fire with them. I'll wait until they get here.' 'Prince, your parents are here!' said Shankhachuda. 'Quickly, cover my body with this cloth! My mother will die if she sees me like this!' Jimutavahana said, trying to hide his bloody, lacerated shoulders and chest where Garuda had ripped away his flesh. 'Ah, my son!' said the old king. 'What kind of compassion is this – that in order to save one Naga from Garuda, you have sacrificed your whole family! We are all ready to die!' 'Oh no!' thought Garuda. 'These are his parents! How can I immolate myself in the fire that they are carrying? But never mind, I am here, at the seashore. I can jump into the submarine fire that has been roaring for ages.'

Jimutavahana tried to rise and greet his parents, but the effort was too much, and he fell back, unconscious. And when they saw him in that condition, the entire family fainted. Garuda, who was now filled with remorse, tried to revive them all by fanning them with his great wings. They recovered slowly, comforting each other, and touching and caressing Jimutavahana in their grief. His mother lamented the state of his formerly beautiful body and unleashed her pain on Garuda. 'Do not grieve for my body, mother,' Jimutavahana sighed. 'It is the same as it was before, just blood and bones and marrow and fat, all covered with skin.' 'Tell me,' pleaded Garuda. 'How do I rid myself of this sin? I am filled with remorse, and I already feel as if I am burning in hell.' 'Listen, and I will tell you,' the prince spoke slowly. 'You must never again take the life of another. Repent for all that you have done before and proceed to create a chain of good deeds that will make up for the past. You will be absolved, and your sin will disappear as would a handful of salt dropped into the ocean.' 'I was asleep, and now I am awakened,' said Garuda. 'I will never kill another living being again. Let the Nagas live in peace and without fear. Let them prosper and play in the underworld and in the ocean as they will!' 'That is good,' said Jimutavahana, his voice getting weaker. 'Now, you, Shankhachuda, go back to your mother and relieve her of her sadness.' 'Would that I were that mother who would see her son again, his body unhurt by Garuda's claws!' the queen wailed. Jimutavahana groaned, 'My body is racked with pain, I am no longer protected from this agony by the good that I did for others. My eyes grow dim, I cannot breathe. But with these last breaths, I ask that I be born again in a body that I can use for the benefit of others!'

There was a great outpouring of grief as Jimutavahana passed out of this life. 'I beg the goddess to revive my son by sprinkling him with the nectar of eternal life!' his mother cried. Garuda realized that he could obtain the elixir for Jimutavahana. 'I will call upon Indra to shower this great being with the nectar of immortality. Not only him but all those Naga men that I have eaten and who are now nothing but a heap of skeletons. And if he refuses, I will dry up the ocean with the power of my wings. I will fly faster and faster through the skies and extinguish the sun. Then I will attack the gods and destroy their weapons – Indra's thunderbolt, Kubera's club and Yama's staff. I will defeat them in battle, and I will shower the elixir on Jimutavahana and the dead Nagas myself!' He flew up into the air and was soon out of sight.

'Child, build a pyre for my son, big enough so that we, too, can go with him,' the old king said to Shankhachuda. Weeping, Shankhachuda built a large pyre. Malayavati climbed onto it along with Jimutavahana's parents. She stood atop the wood and placed her hands together. 'How can it be, dear goddess, that you promised me the lord of the vidyadharas as a husband and yet he lies here lifeless, and I have become a widow!' The goddess Gauri descended from the heavens, carrying a pot in her arms. 'This cannot be, my words can never be untrue,' she said. She sprinkled Jimutavahana's body with water from her pot and immediately, he came back to life. The goddess said, 'I am pleased with you, mighty one, so ready to sacrifice yourself so that another might live.'

The two old people and their son and daughter-in-law, all prostrated themselves at the feet of the goddess and praised her. 'What is this rain that has fallen from a cloudless sky?' wondered the old king. 'Ah, that is the doing of mighty Garuda. He is the reason that Jimutavahana has been restored to life, along with all those Naga kings. Look, they are surrounding Shankhachuda, their jewels bright in their hoods. They are licking up the elixir that has fallen to the ground, they are slithering back into the ocean so that they can reach their homes in the underworld,' replied the goddess. Then she spoke to Jimutavahana. 'And for you, I have more than the gift of life, Jimutavahana. By sprinkling you with this water from the holy Manasa Lake, I have anointed you the universal emperor of all the vidyadharas. I give you these jewels of sovereignty – the golden wheel, the white elephant with the four tusks, the dark-coloured horse and finally, Malayavati herself. Behind them walk all the vidyadhara nobles and chieftains, waving chowrie fans whiter than the autumn moon, bowing low in devotion. Matanga and his men are among them. Is there any other boon I can bestow upon you?' 'There is nothing more that I want,' said Jimutavahana humbly. 'Shankhachuda is alive, Garuda has given up his acts of violence and killing, the Nagas have been brought back to life, my parents are alive and well, and now, our imperial majesty has been restored. All I can ask is that the rains come on time, turning the earth green with bounteous harvests year after year. Let my subjects prosper and with minds free of envy, may they take pleasure in good works and in the company of their families and friends.'

THE LITTLE CLAY CART

BY SHUDRAKA

Mricchakatika is a *prakarana,* a play with an entirely original plot. The heart of the story is a constantly misplaced and purloined box of jewels and it is filled with unforgettable supporting characters, from Maitreya the hero's brahmin companion, to Samsthanaka the king's oafish brother-in-law, to the thief who breaks into homes through holes that he creates as works of art, to Aryaka who leads a revolution of the proletariat and the nameless masseur who becomes a gambler and then a Buddhist monk. There is a love story between an impoverished but very honourable brahmin and the city's finest courtesan that brings all these citizens together in a series of climaxes that make you laugh out loud. The play works as an ode to the city of Ujjain – bustling, cosmopolitan, rowdy, gracious, unforgiving and generous. Its entirely urban setting and flavour make it stand out from other classical Sanskrit plays.

The name Shudraka means 'little servant' and since we have no substantial information about the author, one theory suggests that he was a writer who completed an unfinished play by Bhasa (*Daridra Charudatta*) and signed off on it with this modest moniker suggesting that he was but a footnote, as it were, to the great playwright. Perhaps it was the anonymity that allowed Shudraka to write as he pleased and upturn all the conventions that Sanskrit drama was constrained by – the story is not about kings and chaste young women but revolves around common people who speak an astonishing range of Prakrits, it is determinedly secular in its outlook and the gods are nowhere in sight. Even the title of the play points to the humblest of domestic objects: a child's toy made of mud.

List of Important Characters

Aryaka – leader of the people's revolution
Charudatta – impoverished brahmin who loves Vasantasena
Madanika – Vasantasena's attendant
Maitreya – Charudatta's close friend and companion
Masseur – becomes a gambler and then a Buddhist monk
Radanika – maid in Charudatta's house
Rohasena – Charudatta's son
Samsthanaka – the king's brother-in-law, in love with Vasantasena
Sthavaraka – Samsthanaka's friend
Thief – loyal to Aryaka, in love with Madanika
Vasantasena – courtesan, in love with Charudatta
The captain, the young guard, the judge, the executioners

In the prosperous city of Ujjain, there lived an honourable man named Charudatta, known and beloved among his many friends for his large heart. Charudatta had fallen on bad times and lost his large fortune. Returning home one evening with Maitreya, his constant companion, Charudatta said sadly, 'I do not mourn the loss of wealth, Maitreya. But the fact that my friends have deserted me now that I am poor – that's what makes me sad. Money comes and money goes, I know that, but I would never have thought the same would be true for friends. A man loses respect when he is poor and that leads him to become frustrated and despairing. And there lies the possibility of all evil.' 'Let's change the subject, friend,' said Maitreya. 'This is such a doleful conversation.' Charudatta continued as if he hadn't heard Maitreya. 'A poor man becomes the subject of gossip. Then his friends dismiss him and even strangers speak ill of him. That is my circumstance, and I must find a way to live with it.'

Charudatta paused as he prepared to enter his now somewhat shabby home and turned to Maitreya, saying, 'I have worshipped the household gods already, asking for their favour. Why don't you go to where the four roads meet and ask the gods there to look after us?' 'Absolutely not!' retorted Maitreya sharply. 'If our household gods are not interested in us, I doubt the gods at the crossroads will be. Besides, it's getting dark – all kinds of thugs and bandits will be about, and I know they'll come after a chubby fellow like me. I'm coming in with you . . . ' and he followed Charudatta into the house, still muttering to himself.

In the same city, there lived a beautiful courtesan named Vasantasena. She had many admirers and was well known not only for her skills as a performer but also for her sweet and generous nature. One of Ujjain's most prominent citizens, Samsthanaka, who was the king's brother-in-law, was quite besotted with Vasantasena and showered her with attention even though she had no interest in him. As it happened, that very evening, Samsthanaka and his attendants were pursuing Vasantasena, who tried to get away from them by turning off the main road and into the narrow lanes of the city.

'Stop, Vasantasena, stop!' bellowed Samsthanaka. 'Why do you run from me? You know I love you with all my heart!' His attendants also shouted, 'Vasantasena, why do you run like a deer from a tiger, like a peahen in the monsoon? Your dress is fluttering, your ornaments are jingling. Our lord and master can outrun you any day!' Vasantasena called out to her maids, her voice trembling. 'Who is she calling to?' huffed Samsthanaka. 'Her women servants? Hah! I can fight a hundred women at one time. Watch me!'

Vasantasena realized that she was all alone and that she would have to use her wits to get away from Samsthanaka. 'What do you want from me, good sir? Is it my jewellery?' she asked, trembling. 'Lady, why do you torment me so,' moaned Samsthanaka. 'It's you that I want, it's your love that I want!' 'I am so tired of you, you foolish man!' muttered Vasantasena. One of Samsthanaka's men heard her and said, 'My master is one of the richest and most powerful men in the city. Many women would be happy to love him. Why do you turn him away? Is it because you love that pauper Charudatta? Pah! He has nothing to give a woman like you! He is so poor that he lives on this narrow dark street – his house is somewhere on the left. I'm sure it's the most decrepit one!' 'Ah! Good fortune smiles on me!' Vasantasena whispered to herself. 'The house of the man I love is right here!' Samsthanaka continued to call out, 'Vasanta! Vasantasena! Damn this darkness, I can't see her! How will I find her?' 'My lord, stop shouting and listen for the sound of her anklets. They will lead you to her,' said one of his companions. Immediately, Vasantasena took off her anklets and other ornaments and crept up against a wall as she tried to find the door of Charudatta's house.

Inside the house, with barely enough oil to light a lamp, Charudatta had finished his evening worship. Again, he asked Maitreya to pray for him at the crossroads, and this time, Maitreya agreed on condition that he could take Radanika, the maid, with him. Telling Radanika to hold onto the package with all the materials needed for the prayer ritual, Maitreya proceeded to open the back door. As he turned away after unlocking the door, Vasantasena slipped into the house unnoticed.

Maitreya and Radanika set off on their task, but they ran into Samsthanaka and his men. 'There she is!' shouted Samsthanaka, and he grabbed Radanika by her hair. 'Maitreya!' shrieked Radanika. 'Help! Some awful man has caught hold of me!' Maitreya waved his stick around, acting braver than he was feeling. Then he recognized Samsthanaka. 'Ugh!' he exclaimed. 'You are that horrid fellow, the king's brother-in-law and the scourge of all the women in Ujjain! How dare you try and break into Charudatta's house – he is the most noble of all Ujjain's citizens, even if he is one of the poorest! How dare you attack the people who work for him!'

Samsthanaka's attendant rushed up to apologize. 'We were looking for another girl, sir. My master has mistaken your companion for her. Truly, we meant no harm. Please, sir, don't tell noble Charudatta what has just happened,' he begged, bowing low before Maitreya. 'Idiot!' shouted Samsthanaka. 'Why are you grovelling in front of this fat fool?' 'Because I am afraid of Charudatta's virtue,' said the attendant. 'Scared? Of an impoverished man? What sense does that make?' blustered Samsthanaka. 'His virtues make him rich,' said the attendant. 'He has been generous and kind, a patron of scholars, a learned man himself. He has lived life fully, while people like us, we only exist. Come, let us go.' Samsthanaka turned to Maitreya and said, 'You tell your virtuous master – that useless man who has no money and no power nor any stature in this city – you tell him that that lowlife woman Vasantasena has hidden herself in his house because she thinks she is in love with him. Tell him to return her to me without any fuss and nonsense. If I have to go to the police to get her back, he will regret it. He will have no enemy worse than me!' He shook his fist in front of Maitreya's face and continued, 'You make sure he gets this message, mister!' Maitreya assured Samsthanaka that the message would reach Charudatta and taking Radanika by the arm, he hurried off, muttering, 'Let's not tell Charudatta any of this, Radanika. The poor man has enough troubles as it is!'

Unaware of the ruckus in the street, Charudatta saw someone standing by the door inside the house and said, 'Ah, Radanika, you're still here. Please bring little Rohasena indoors. It's getting cool and he might catch a cold. Here, take this shawl for him.' He drew the shawl he was wearing from his shoulders and handed it to the woman. 'He thinks I'm the maid,' thought Vasantasena as she quietly took the shawl that Charudatta held out to her. 'Oh, he is a lovely man, so gentle, so kind. And what is this perfume he uses? The shawl smells so sweet.' She said nothing aloud. Charudatta sighed, 'Radanika doesn't answer. Well, even my friends don't talk to me now that I'm poor.'

Just then, Maitreya and Radanika returned. Startled, Charudatta burst out, 'Radanika? But then, who is this lady? How rude of me to have been so familiar with her! She is like the moon half hidden in the clouds. O dear, how can I speak like this to her? She is surely the respected wife of another man!' Maitreya interrupted him. 'She is not the wife of another man. She is Vasantasena, the courtesan who fell in love with you when she saw you at the temple. I have a message for you from the king's brother-in-law. He says you should hand her back to him without any fuss or else he will be your sworn enemy!' Charudatta thought to himself, 'What an amazing woman! She has chosen me over that rich and powerful man!' But aloud, he said, 'My apologies, good lady, for mistaking you for Radanika and speaking to you so casually!' 'It is I who must apologize to you for entering your house uninvited,' replied Vasantasena, thinking all the while what a good man Charudatta was. 'I must not take advantage of you, but please, may I leave my jewels here? Those thugs were trying to rob me when I escaped.' 'You shall have them back whenever you want them, My Lady,' said Charudatta. 'Take the jewels, Maitreya, and escort the lady back to her home.'

Soon after this, Vasantasena's companion, Madanika, noticed her looking pale and out of sorts. She said, 'You're very absent-minded these days. Are you in love?' Vasantasena laughed. 'You are so perceptive!' 'Madam, is it the man you met at the temple that has captured your heart? I've heard he's poor.' 'But I love him,' protested Vasantasena. 'At least people won't think that I am attracted to his money!' 'When will you visit him?' asked Madanika. 'After all, you did leave your jewels at his house. Do you have a plan?' 'I most certainly do!' smiled Vasantasena.

In another part of the city, a masseur was running away from a group of gamblers. He had lost a lot of money to those seasoned players and had no way of paying back the ten gold coins that he owed them. He ran into a nearby temple, and when he saw that the temple had no idol, he decided to stand there, motionless, as if he were the idol of the deity. The men who had been chasing him noticed that his footprints had stopped just in front of the temple and they followed him in. Unable to see him anywhere, they settled down for one last game before they called it a night and went home. The masseur could not resist the rattle and roll of the dice and he leapt forward, shouting, 'My turn! My turn!' The gamblers fell upon him and demanded their money. The masseur pleaded he had no money, nothing even to sell, unless he was to sell himself. The gamblers led the masseur to the market and tried to sell him for ten pieces of gold. When no one was interested, they started to beat him.

A passer-by named Darduraka, who had an old enmity with the gamblers, intervened and helped the masseur escape. The masseur took to his heels and fled, entering the first open door he saw. Fortunately for him, the house he entered was Vasantasena's. He threw himself at her feet when he saw her, crying, 'Help me! Help me!' 'You have nothing to fear,' she said gently. 'What is the problem?' 'I owe a man some money,' stammered the masseur. Madanika said, 'Sir, my mistress wishes to know who you are and why you are here and what you are afraid of.' 'I am from the city of Pataliputra. My father taught me the art of massage and that's how I make my living. I wanted to see the world, and so I made my way here, to this great city of Ujjain, and found a job with the kindest, the best of all men. He was so well-bred and so handsome, he was so generous and cared for his friends and his enemies alike.' 'I think I know this man,' said Vasantasena to herself. 'That man, he gave away so much of his wealth . . . ' Interrupting the masseur, she said, ' . . . he has nothing left.' 'Ah, you know him,' said the masseur happily. 'Who has not heard of him, my sweet and gentle master, Charudatta! But I had to leave him when he lost his money and could no longer pay me. I became a gambler to make a living. And I've just lost ten gold pieces!'

Suddenly, there was a great commotion outside the house. A man was shouting about having been cheated and robbed. 'That's him, madam, the man that I owe money to! What shall I do?' cried the masseur. Vasantasena took off one of the bracelets she was wearing and said to Madanika, 'Give this to that fellow and tell him it has come from our friend here.' The gambler was more than pleased to take the gem-studded bracelet in place of the ten gold pieces. Madanika came back and reported the success of her mission. The masseur announced he was giving up both the massage business and gambling. He was going to repent and become a Buddhist monk.

At that moment, Karnapuraka, Vasantasena's retainer, rushed into the room, full of excitement and out of breath. 'Madam, madam, I wish you had been there to see how brave I was! Your elephant got loose and killed its keeper and ran out onto the main street, and people started shouting and screaming and running about, and climbing into trees, but the elephant kept coming, smashing and breaking things, and then a holy man who was begging came along, and the elephant went after him and crushed his begging bowl and cracked his staff, and then the man was caught between the elephant's legs and everyone was screaming, "Oh! He'll be killed . . . he's dead already!" And then . . . wait, don't interrupt . . . I grabbed an iron bar from a shop, charged at the elephant and hit it with all my might. The iron bar pierced the elephant and it collapsed in a heap, right there, and I, I saved the holy man! People gathered and showered praises on me, and then a man, I don't know who, threw his shawl over me!' 'How very brave you have been,' said Vasantasena. 'But does that shawl smell of jasmine?' she asked eagerly. 'I can only smell elephant,' replied Karnapuraka, 'but it has his name written on it.' 'Charudatta!' sighed Vasantasena as she read the name and pulled the shawl around herself. She gave a jewel to Karnapuraka. 'Where is he, now?' she asked. 'He was going home. He should be passing by on this road any minute,' said Karnapuraka. Vasantasena took Madanika by the hand and ran to the balcony, hoping for a glimpse of Charudatta as he went by.

Later, Charudatta and Maitreya were returning from a concert that Charudatta had enjoyed very much. Maitreya was less pleased, and as they walked along, he complained on and on about the singer and his voice. When they reached Charudatta's house, they woke the servant who had been asleep and told him to fetch water so that they could wash their feet. The servant, Vardhamanaka, said to Maitreya, 'Please take this golden box which I've been guarding all day. It's night now, so it's your turn to look after it.' Maitreya took it, grumbling that he would have to stay up all night to keep an eye on the box. 'I'll just put it away,' he said. 'No, you will not,' said Charudatta firmly. 'It has been left in our care and must be safely returned to its owner.' Maitreya set the box beside him, and soon the household was fast asleep.

A thief was on the prowl that night in the neighbourhood, and he chose Charudatta's house to break into. Carefully, he made a hole in the outer wall of the house and crept in, noticing that there were two men sleeping in the courtyard. He looked around in the dim light of his candle and saw that there was nothing to steal. As he was about to leave, Maitreya muttered in his sleep, speaking to Charudatta, 'I can see a hole in the wall. There's a thief in here. You better hang onto this box of jewels.' The thief froze. After a few moments, he realized that Maitreya was talking in his sleep. 'Oh dear, this fellow seems like a poor man. How can I take what little he has?' thought the thief. But Maitreya spoke again. 'Take it, please, take it!' The thief felt a pang of remorse as he reached for the box that Maitreya held out. 'Look what I've come to,' he thought to himself. 'I'm an educated man, and here I am, reduced to being a common thief. And it's all for the woman I love, Madanika! Now I can go to Vasantasena and buy my beloved's freedom.'

The thief slipped away, but not before he was spotted by Radanika, who raised the alarm, waking both Maitreya and Charudatta with her screams. Charudatta said, 'Well, that thief must be new to the city – he's probably the only person who doesn't know that there's nothing to steal in my house.' Maitreya quickly agreed, 'He must have hoped for a box of jewels at least. You call me a fool but thank heavens I handed that box of jewels over to you in the middle of the night.' 'What box?' sputtered Charudatta. 'The one we were supposed to keep safe,' said Maitreya. Charudatta fainted when he heard Maitreya's words. Maitreya splashed his face with water, but when Charudatta recovered, he was in tears. 'We are finished Maitreya, finished!' Charudatta wept. 'Everyone will think that I stole the jewels! Oh, I curse my poverty! It has finally caught up even with my good name!'

Radanika had rushed into the inner rooms to tell her mistress about the theft. Charudatta's wife understood that her husband would be shamed by what had happened. She called Maitreya and gave him her last piece of jewellery: a magnificent double strand of pearls. 'Let my husband use this to replace the value of what has been stolen from our care,' she said. Maitreya was embarrassed by her goodness and blessed her before he took the pearls to Charudatta and told him what his wife had said. Charudatta burst into a fresh bout of tears, saying, 'How can I call myself poor when I have such a loving wife and a good friend who is always by my side! Maitreya, go immediately to Vasantasena's house and tell her that we forgot the jewels were hers and gambled them away, and that I send her this necklace instead. Do not return until you have placed this necklace in her hands.' Maitreya went off, grumbling to himself.

Vasantasena had just received two messages at once – one from her mother asking her to visit and another telling her that Samsthanaka had sent her ten thousand gold pieces and a carriage to bring her to him. Vasantasena was not interested in either of the invitations and flounced off into the inner apartments. She opened a window and saw Madanika talking to a man. 'She looks quite in love with him,' thought Vasantasena. 'I think I should try and hear what they're talking about.' The man, who was the thief from the night before, told Madanika that he had managed to put together the price of her freedom. He assured her that he had done nothing more than steal and had committed even this crime out of his love for her. He showed her the jewels and said she should give them to her mistress. Madanika remarked that they looked familiar and asked him where he had got them. Very reluctantly, the thief admitted that he had taken them from Charudatta's house. 'You fool!' cried Madanika. 'These are Vasantasena's ornaments. She had left them at Charudatta's house!' 'How was I supposed to know that?' retorted the thief. 'What do we do now?' 'Give them back, of course,' said Madanika, firmly. 'They'll imprison me!' said the thief. 'If I return them, it'll prove that I stole them. I can't do that! Think of some other solution!' 'All right,' Madanika replied, thinking for a moment. 'I'll say to my mistress you're from Charudatta's house and that you've brought her jewels back.' Madanika hurried away.

Vasantasena took the jewels the thief held out to her, and as he turned to leave, she said, 'Wait, I have something for you. Take Madanika. Charudatta and I had an agreement that whoever brought the jewels to me would get this lovely girl as a gift. So, take her with you and please convey my thanks to Charudatta.' She turned to Madanika. 'Go child, go to your new life with your lover. But do think of me now and then.' Madanika and the thief bowed to Vasantasena, thanking her profusely. They left the house and climbed into the carriage that was waiting outside.

Just then, the town crier came by, announcing that an astrologer had predicted that Aryaka, the son of a cowherd, would become king, and Aryaka had, therefore, been arrested and put in prison. 'This is just a warning!' shouted the crier as he passed through the street. The thief was startled and jumped out of the carriage. 'Aryaka? He's my friend! I can't possibly enjoy any wedding celebrations. I must get in touch with all our friends who have suffered under this tyrant king. How can Aryaka be imprisoned for doing nothing? This is the act of a spineless coward!' 'But what about me!' wailed Madanika. 'I'll be with you shortly,' said the thief. 'Coachman! Do you know the way to the house of the musician Rebhila? Take my woman there at once. I'll be back as soon as I can,' he said and disappeared.

Meanwhile, a maid announced to Vasantasena that a messenger named Maitreya had arrived from Charudatta. Vasantasena told the maid to usher him in with all courtesies and honours. The maid led Maitreya through the beautiful and well-appointed courtyards of Vasantasena's house, eight in number. His eyes nearly fell out of his head at the beauty and opulence around him. He marvelled at the balconies and the ponds and the well-fed domestic cattle and the other animals – peacocks and deer and parrots –kept as pets, and admired the spaces for performance, the separate rooms for musicians to live and practise in, the vast kitchens and finally, the inner apartments where Vasantasena's family lived.

Vasantasena herself was seated in a secluded garden, lush with flowering plants and trees heavy with fruit, filled with birdsong and the humming of bees. When she saw Maitreya, she welcomed him and asked warmly after Charudatta. Doing his best to maintain his dignity, Maitreya said, 'Madam, Charudatta asked me to tell you that he lost your box of jewels at a gambling game and is unable to retrieve it at the moment. In place of what has been lost, he asks you to accept this double string of pearls.' Vasantasena said to herself, 'Oh, he is too proud to tell me the jewels have been stolen.

I love him even more for that!' She held out her hand for the pearls and said aloud, 'Thank you. Tell Charudatta that I will visit him this evening.' Maitreya bowed and left. Vasantasena turned to her maid and said, 'Take this necklace and prepare to come with me to Charudatta's house.'

Maitreya muttered and mumbled all the way back to Charudatta's house, complaining about Vasantasena's lack of hospitality and how she had greedily accepted the valuable necklace in exchange for a box full of tawdry gold ornaments which had, in any case, been stolen.

Charudatta was sitting in a pavilion in his garden, enjoying the beauty of the rain and the storm clouds streaked with lightning. Maitreya announced that Vasantasena had arrived, and Charudatta rose from his seat, delighted to welcome her. 'Good evening, Mr Gambler,' Vasantasena greeted Charudatta playfully. Charudatta saw that she was drenched and immediately sent her maid into the house with Maitreya to fetch some dry garments. 'Why are you here?' asked Maitreya quite rudely. 'Let me tell you,' said the maid. 'My mistress is here to find out the value of the necklace. You see, she gambled it away and the man she lost it to has gone out of town. For now, she would like you to accept this box of jewels as recompense.' She held out the very box the thief had given Vasantasena in exchange for Madanika's freedom.

Maitreya frowned at the trick that was being played on them, but Charudatta was overjoyed and wanted to reward the maid for the good news with a ring from his finger. His hands, however, were bare, and once again, Charudatta commented sadly on his misfortune. Vasantasena said sweetly, 'There was no need for you to send me the necklace, Charudatta. You have demeaned me by doing so!' 'Who would ever have believed the truth?' cried Charudatta. Maitreya interrupted and said to Vasantasena, 'The storm has become more fierce. Are you, by any chance, planning to stay the night here?' Oblivious to everything except the presence of Vasantasena and the magnificent storm that filled the skies with the rumble of thunder and streaks of lightning, Charudatta spontaneously composed and recited a poem about the passions that the storm aroused in the human heart. Unable to resist any longer, Vasantasena embraced him and Charudatta took her into his arms.

The next morning, Vasantasena tried to return the pearl necklace to Charudatta's wife, who refused, politely but firmly. She sent it back along with a message that the only ornament she valued was her virtuous husband. Before Vasantasena could respond, Charudatta's little son wandered into her chamber, for she had, indeed, spent the night at Charudatta's house. The child was followed by the maid of the house, who was trying to distract him with his toys. 'Here,' she said, 'play with this little clay cart!' 'I don't want a clay cart,' the boy replied angrily, as he stamped his feet. 'I want a golden cart, full of toys!' 'Who is this young gentleman,' asked Vasantasena. 'He's Charudatta's son,' said the maid, tartly. 'But why is he so upset?' 'His friend was given a gold cart the other day and now he wants one too. I made him this clay one, but as you can see, he doesn't care for it.'

'Come here, child,' said Vasantasena, smiling as she picked the boy up and sat him in her lap. 'Who are you?' he asked. 'I came to see your father,' she replied. 'She is a friend of your mother's,' said the maid quickly. 'No, she isn't,' said the boy as he took in Vasantasena's glittering appearance. 'She's wearing so many golden things. My mother does not dress like this.' Vasantasena burst into tears and filled the boy's cart with her jewels. 'Take these, little one. Go and buy yourself a cart made of gold.' Her maid whispered that Charudatta was waiting for her in the botanical garden and had sent a conveyance to bring her there. Vasantasena hurriedly left the house with her maid.

Charudatta's coachman had been waiting outside, but suddenly, he realized that he had forgotten the seat cushions. Not wanting to leave his carriage unattended, he decided to fetch the cushions himself, expecting to be back in time to take his special passenger to the gardens.

A great commotion broke out on the street as he drove off – crowds of people, carts and animals appeared as if from nowhere, and soon there was barely room to move. As it happened, Sthavaraka, Samsthanaka's good friend, was driving his carriage through that very street and ran right into the crowds. 'What a bother,' he thought to himself as he pulled over to the side. 'I wonder where all these villagers have come from. I'll just wait here, outside Charudatta's gate, until this mess clears.'

Vasantasena came out and saw a carriage waiting. She dismissed her maid and climbed into the back without alerting the driver. Sthavaraka had grown impatient and he could see that whatever was happening was not going to sort itself out in a hurry. Suddenly he heard someone shouting in the distance, 'Police! Police! The traitor has escaped, he has killed the jailer! Guards! Man your posts!' So Sthavaraka drove off quickly to his appointment with Samsthanaka, who was also heading towards the botanical garden.

No one noticed a man with chains on his feet melt into the milling crowd. It was Aryaka who cursed under his breath. 'All this, this captivity, these chains, this suffering – all this is due to that villain Palaka, the man who rules this kingdom. But it's behind me now, even if I have to drag these chains around. My freedom was given to me by my friend, the thief, who got me out of prison. I wish him well. That coward Palaka – he took everything I had, because he was afraid of a stupid prophecy. If all this is fated, if this is what is to be, how is it my fault? Why am I being punished!' As Aryaka looked around for a place to hide, he saw a broken gate hanging off its hinges. 'Poor fellow, who cannot even repair his gate. But his misfortune is to my benefit!' he thought, as he slipped into the courtyard.

Soon enough, Charudatta's carriage rolled into the courtyard, and the coachman called for the maid to fetch Vasantasena. 'My master is waiting in the botanical garden!' he shouted. Aryaka could not believe his luck. 'Amazing! An empty carriage that's heading out of the city! What more could I ask for!' He clambered into the back. The coachman heard the clatter of his chains and said, 'Ah! The jingling of anklets! My lady must have seated herself. Off we go!' And he drove the carriage out onto the street.

Meanwhile, the king's guards were swarming all over the place. Their captain shouted, 'Don't let that traitor escape again! Look everywhere! Examine every man you see! Look inside all the carts and carriages!' They stopped Charudatta's carriage and one of the guards said roughly, 'And where do you think you're going? Who are you? Who is in there?' 'Sir, please, this is Charudatta's carriage and I'm taking Vasantasena to meet him in the gardens outside the city,' said the coachman confidently. 'Let him pass,' said the captain. 'Charudatta and Vasantasena are both well-respected citizens.' But the young guard stood his ground. 'I don't know who they are. And you said we have to inspect every cart, every carriage. I'm not going to let this carriage move until you go and see who's in there.' The captain realized that he had to set an example. He marched to the back and drew open the curtain. Aryaka looked him in the eye and said softly, 'Do not betray me!' The captain thought to himself, 'He's a good man, and I know he's not guilty. Besides, that thief who got him out saved my life once. Any friend of his is a friend of mine.' He quietly passed his sword to Aryaka and said loudly, 'A passport for your safe passage through the city, My Lady Vasantasena!'

Coming around to the front, the captain slapped the horse on the rump and said, 'Off you go! Tell anyone who dares to stop you that the carriage has been inspected by me, the captain, in the presence of my men.' But the younger guard was having none of this. 'I am a servant of the king. I have been told to search every carriage and you cannot stop me!' The captain knew that Charudatta would be in danger if Aryaka was found in his carriage. 'You challenge me?' he shouted. 'You, you low caste fellow! How dare you!' 'What do you mean?' demanded the guard.

'Everyone knows your family works with leather, you touch the skins of dead animals, you sew them like this and like this!' the captain said, gesturing rudely. 'And you? You're a tanner!' spat the guard. 'Your family has worked with drums so long that they are all like them – your mother is a drum, your father is a bigger drum, your brother is a big fat drum, your sister . . . !' 'Shut up!' the captain cried as he swung his fist at the guard. They began to fight, and the captain kicked the younger man. 'Oh ho ho! You kicked me! I'm going to complain about you in the court of law! You'll be whipped!' 'That's right, go and complain, you coward!'

The guard went off in a huff, and the captain urged Charudatta's coachman to hurry on.

At the garden, Charudatta was waiting impatiently with Maitreya, fretting and wondering why the carriage and his beloved were so delayed. When the carriage finally arrived, Charudatta ran to help Vasantasena alight. But when he opened the curtain, he fell back in surprise. 'Maitreya! This is a man – strong and well-built, with fierce eyes. And look! My goodness, there are chains on his feet!' Aryaka shrewdly assessed Charudatta and decided that this was a good man, noble and true. 'I am Aryaka,' he said, simply. 'I am a herdsman. I need your help.' 'Are you the one that the king arrested because he feared an astrologer's prediction?' Charudatta could barely control his incredulity. 'My friend, fate has brought you here. You can ask me for anything. Coachman, take these chains off his feet.'

Aryaka bowed and thanked Charudatta. 'Please don't misunderstand. I am grateful for your help, but I need to leave immediately.' 'Of course,' replied Charudatta. 'But you're not going to get anywhere very quickly on foot. Why don't you keep the carriage? No one will bother you if you are in there!' Aryaka left in the carriage and Charudatta reconciled himself to the fact that he was not going to see Vasantasena that day. He and Maitreya set off for home. 'O dear!' said Charudatta. 'There's a Buddhist monk coming this way. That's a bad omen. And my left eye has been twitching, which does not bode well, either. Let's avoid him by taking another path.'

The Buddhist monk was none other than the masseur-turned-gambler who had forsworn the fickle dice after his last encounter with unforgiving creditors. He walked along, singing merrily about the Buddhist virtues of poverty and chastity and renouncing the pleasures of the senses. 'Ah, I have reached the pleasure garden of my friend Samsthanaka. And what a lovely little pond this is,' he said as he ended his happy song. He looked around. 'This is a good place to wash my new monk's robe.' From the corner of his eye, the monk saw a large man charging towards him, cursing and swearing. An attendant was running behind him, trying to restrain him from attacking the monk. But the man, who was none other than Samsthanaka, rained blows on the monk, berating him for washing clothes in a pond that belonged to him, the king's brother-in-law. The attendant tried to distract him. 'Look, sir, look at this beautiful garden with these flowering trees and all the lovely birds. Listen, and you will hear their sweet song. Come, let us sit on this bench in the shade and enjoy the gentle breeze. Come, come!' But Samsthanaka was in no mood to be cajoled. 'It's so hot! Where is my carriage? Why is that fool Sthavaraka taking so long to get here? Uff, I am hot! Do something!' The attendant led him to the bench and fanned him with some large leaves, but Samsthanaka ranted on. 'You know, I haven't been able to forget that Vasantasena. How could she insult me like that? How could she not be interested in me? I'll show her who I really am. Just wait till I see her again.'

Even as he was speaking, his carriage drew up to the gates of his garden. The gates were quite narrow, but Samsthanaka insisted that Sthavaraka pass through them and come into the garden. Sthavaraka was annoyed, worrying that the carriage might be damaged or that he might be hurt, but he knew he had no chance to express his opinion or do what he thought was best and so, he crashed the carriage through the gates. Samsthanaka hurried to the back to see if there had been any damage. 'Oh, oh, I am finished!'

he yelled as he ran back to his companions. 'Save me! There's a witch in there! Get her out, get this woman out!' His attendant sauntered over to the back and pulled open the carriage curtain. 'Vasantasena!' he said smiling. 'What are you doing here? The last time we met, you were so superior, such a snob – we were not good enough for the likes of you. And, now, here you are! Is it the money that tempts you? Are these your mother's instructions, my dear courtesan?' 'No, no, it's not like that!' she cried. 'This is all a mistake! This is the wrong carriage! . . . Please, you must help me!' The attendant turned away and went back to where the others were. 'Hey, you're alive!' said Samsthanaka. 'I was sure that witch would eat you up!' 'It's Vasantasena in the carriage, sir!' said the attendant. Samsthanaka almost danced with joy. 'She has come to me, you see! She has come to me! I am irresistible! The last time we met, I made her angry, but this time I will beg her forgiveness. She will succumb to my charms – just you watch!'

Samsthanaka ran back and threw himself at Vasantasena's feet. 'Good lady, please forgive my bad manners at our last meeting. Here I am, your servant, your slave!' 'Get away!' Vasantasena cried and kicked at him with her foot. Enraged, Samsthanaka turned on Sthavaraka. 'Where did you pick up this woman, this horrible creature? Did you think you would please me?' 'My lord,' said Sthavaraka, 'I was stuck in a crowd and had to wait in the street where Charudatta lives. This woman must have sneaked into my carriage while I was helping a villager get his cart out of the mud.' 'So, she wasn't coming to meet me! She had an appointment with that penniless brahmin lover of hers! First she turns me down and now she kicks me! She'll die for this!' Samsthanaka ranted on as his attendant helped Vasantasena alight from the carriage. 'Come,

I'll give you whatever you want – money, jewels, power – if you kill her!' he said. His men stared at him, aghast, when they realized that he was serious. Sthavaraka drove off in a great hurry, not wanting to be involved in whatever ensued.

But when Samsthanaka lunged at Vasantasena and tried to grab her, the other attendant restrained him. 'Let me go, you idiot! I was only frightening her,' gasped Samsthanaka. 'I mean no harm, I love her! Why don't you go after Sthavaraka and bring him back? I'm going to need my carriage.' With some reluctance, the attendant moved away. After all, it was hard to believe that the king's brother-in-law, this besotted man, would actually harm the object of his affections.

Samsthanaka plucked some flowers and adorned himself. He minced over to where Vasantasena was cowering, utterly bewildered by all that was going on around her. 'Come here, darling, my sweet love,' cooed Samsthanaka. 'Let me shower you with gold, let me cover you with it.' 'Gold! You think I want gold? And from you? Get away from me, you fat fool!' 'Still choosing that pauper Charudatta over me, are you? He can't come to help you, not even now when you are going to die!' Samsthanaka struck Vasantasena and grabbed her by the neck, intending to strangle her. Vasantasena fell to the ground, unconscious. 'Hah! That was easy. I didn't actually do anything,' Samsthanaka muttered to himself. 'But I should hide this body. And myself.' He dragged Vasantasena's body behind some bushes just as his attendant returned with Sthavaraka.

'Where is she?' asked the attendant, looking around for Vasantasena. 'She's gone,' replied Samsthanaka. 'She must have followed you.' 'No, she didn't,' said the attendant. 'Which way did she go?' The more he questioned Samsthanaka, the more agitated he became and the more hollow the story sounded. Finally, Samsthanaka burst out, 'All right, all right, I killed her!' and showed them the body. The attendant quickly realized that this murder was going to be blamed on him. He fled as fast as he could, having made up his mind to join his friend, the thief, and the others who seemed to be up to something big. Samsthanaka insisted that Sthavaraka, who was still there, take all his jewels and ornaments and leave immediately with the carriage, he promised to join him later. Puzzled, Sthavaraka left.

'I'll take care of that idiot attendant the moment I get to the king's palace,' said Samsthanaka to himself. 'This secret of mine will be safe. But first, I must make sure that that silly cow is really dead. Otherwise, I'm going to have to do this all over again.' He went over to the body and nudged it with his foot. 'She looks pretty dead. I'll cover her with these dry leaves so that she's hidden. And now, I'll go to the courts and say that Charudatta killed Vasantasena in the botanical garden for her money. Aha! I'm a clever fellow! This is a very good way to get rid of Charudatta.' He looked up and saw the monk coming towards him. 'Damn, there's that monk. He hates me because I've beaten him up in the past. If he sees me with this body, he'll say I killed her. I'd better get out of here.' Samsthanaka managed to haul himself over the garden wall and disappeared.

The monk ambled along, still singing his songs of Buddhist virtue, looking for a place to dry the robe he had just washed. He was thinking about Vasantasena's kindness in saving him from the gamblers when he hears a sound from the bushes. He went over to investigate and was shocked to see Vasantasena herself, gasping for water. He gently placed his wet robe over her face and she began to revive. The monk told her who he was and how she had saved him, and when Vasantasena remembered him, he persuaded her to come with him to a nearby Buddhist commune of nuns where she would be taken care of and could recover slowly.

Meanwhile, Samsthanaka had bathed and changed his clothes and arrived at the city's law courts, demanding to be heard because he was the king's brother-in-law. The judge told the clerk to let him know that the courts were very busy that day. Samsthanaka began to shout about all the important people he knew and how he would make the judge's life miserable if he were not heard at once. The judge sighed and thought it best not to antagonize the vain and vengeful man. 'Aha! I have my turn after all,' said Samsthanaka. 'Good judge, let me tell you that I am a noble man from a good family. The king is my sister's husband, my brother-in-law, my father is his father-in-law, I am very well connected . . . ' 'Yes,' interrupted the judge. 'I am sure you are. But do you have a case to present?' 'I do, I do!' replied Samsthanaka rubbing his hands together with glee. 'I went early this morning to the botanical garden and what do you think I saw there? The body of a woman! Do you know who it was? Vasantasena, the city's most expensive courtesan! Clearly some vile chap had lured her there and then strangled her for her ornaments. I didn't see it happen . . . ' 'How did you know that she had been strangled and that she had been killed for her jewels?' asked the judge sharply. 'Huh! I could see the marks on her neck, and she was not wearing any jewellery!' 'Very well,' said the judge. 'But I must consider the evidence as well as the allegations before I decide the case. Bring Vasantasena's mother here,' he said to his clerk.

The mother was brought to the courthouse and questioned

gently by the judge. 'Do you know where your daughter is?' 'She went to visit a friend last night and I have not seen her today.' 'Who was that friend?' Vasantasena's mother looked at the ground, embarrassed. 'You must answer the judge!' urged the clerk. The mother hesitated, 'He is a good man, the son of Sagaradatta. His name is Charudatta, and he lives . . . ' 'Charudatta! Charudatta! He is the murderer!' shouted Samsthanaka. 'Bring in this Charudatta,' ordered the judge, and Charudatta was duly summoned. 'Do you know the courtesan Vasantasena? Is she your friend?' Charudatta's face turned red. 'How can I say that a courtesan is my friend?' he wondered. 'This is a court of law,' said the judge sternly. 'You must tell the truth. There is a charge against you.' 'I charge you with murder. You killed Vasantasena for her jewels!' said Samsthanaka, beside himself with excitement. 'Ignore him,' continued the judge. 'Is she your friend?' 'Yes,' said Charudatta. 'Do you know where she is now?' 'All I can say is that she left my house,' Charudatta spoke softly. 'That's it, eh?' bellowed Samsthanaka. 'Nothing about asking her to meet you at the garden so that you could steal her jewels and kill her!' 'That's not true!' cried Vasantasena's mother. 'I know she left a box of jewels in his care to keep them safe and they were stolen from his house. He gave her a very valuable necklace in exchange. Why would a man like this rob her? And kill her?'

Just then, a soldier from the king's guard burst into the courtroom. 'I said I would go to court to complain! Sir, good judge, you know that Aryaka has escaped and that we are all looking for him. That captain, he kicked me. He mocked me and abused me! I told him I wanted to look inside a carriage he had already inspected and he stopped me. I was doing my job, sir, and he kicked me!' 'Whose carriage was it?' asked the judge. 'Do you know?' 'Yes, sir!

It belongs to this man here, this Charudatta. Vasantasena was in it and she was going to meet him in the botanical garden.' 'Not a good day for Charudatta,' the judge muttered to himself. 'Captain, go the garden and see if there's a woman's body there!'

The captain returned with the news that there was, indeed, a woman's body in the garden and that animals had been at it. 'It's best you tell the truth, Charudatta,' said the judge. 'You all know me,' said Charudatta, who was now quite agitated. 'You know I don't like even to pluck flowers from their vines. Why would I kill Vasantasena? You believe the word of this crazy fellow, this man who has no control over his impulses, his emotions! What will Maitreya think of me? And my dear, good wife? And my little boy – what does he even know of life and death?' He looked around nervously and said to himself, 'Where is that Maitreya? I had told him to return the jewels Vasantasena had given my son. Why is he so late?'

Just then, Maitreya stumbled into the courtroom. He had been stopped on his errand and told that Charudatta had been called to court and so he had hurried over. 'What is going on?' he panted. 'Why are you here?' he asked Charudatta. 'This man, Samsthanaka,' said Charudatta, 'has accused me of murdering Vasantasena and stealing her jewels.' Maitreya could not believe his ears. He turned on the judge. 'You think this gentle person, this man of generosity and kindness, would kill Vasantasena? Would kill anyone? He's donated to the public good and to all kinds of charities, and he's made himself a pauper as a result! And you, Samsthanaka, you apology for a human being, you scoundrel, you lecher, you villain! I'm going to kill you, you fat oaf!' Samsthanaka came forward and struck Maitreya, who hit him back. As they scuffled, the bundle of jewels fell from Maitreya's clothing onto the floor. Charudatta groaned and buried his head in his hands. 'Are these your daughter's jewels?' the clerk asked Vasantasena's mother. 'No! These are poor imitations!' she said firmly.

'Are they yours, Charudatta?' 'They are not. They belong to Vasantasena. I cannot tell you how she lost them, but I can tell you that they were taken from my house,' said Charudatta. 'Say that you have killed her!' cried Samsthanaka. 'You have said it for me,' Charudatta said bitterly. He was utterly without hope. 'I cannot help you. I must declare you guilty,' said the judge. 'Sentence will be passed by the king, but you know that since you are a brahmin, you will be banished from the kingdom. Clerk, go tell the king the facts of the case.' When the clerk returned, the news was not good. Charudatta was to be executed at the old burial ground as a warning to all those who contemplated murder. He was marched away by the guards.

Charudatta was led through the street in chains and his crime was proclaimed aloud for all to hear. He hung his head in shame as his high caste and reputation as a good man and one of Ujjain's most prominent citizens was replaced by the infamy of a thief and a murderer. He was distraught that none of his friends had come to comfort him, and he begged his executioners, who appeared to be kind and cheerful despite their unpleasant profession, to let him see his son before he was executed. Maitreya brought the little boy to see his father, who had nothing to give his son as a memento. Suddenly, a man broke through the crowd that had gathered. It was Sthavaraka. 'Stop! Stop! Charudatta is innocent! Listen to me! I am the one who brought Vasantasena to the botanical garden. She had climbed into my carriage by mistake. Charudatta was not present, and it was Samsthanaka, my master, who strangled her because she had spurned him as a suitor.' But no one was ready to take Sthavaraka's version of the story as the truth because he had no proof.

Samsthanaka showed up to revel in Charudatta's misfortune and watch him being beheaded. But the executioners seemed to be in no hurry to finish their assignment. 'It's your turn today,' said one to the other. 'Nope, I did the last one, this one's yours,' the other replied. 'Come on, come on! You have the king's orders. Do your job!' shouted Samsthanaka. 'What's the rush? Someone might come by and save him – it's been known to happen, a sudden stroke of good fortune. Someone might buy his freedom, or the king might have a son and declare a general pardon. An elephant might get loose and create a great commotion. There could be a new king, even . . . ' said one of the executioners. 'New king? What do you mean? That's rubbish!' growled Samsthanaka. The executioner continued as if there had been no interruption. 'You see, that's why I never hurry. Give a man a good chance to escape the gallows.' 'We beg your forgiveness, noble Charudatta,' said the other. 'We are only following the king's orders. But the time is drawing near and we are close to the execution ground. I can see the vultures and the jackals.' Charudatta shuddered but walked on.

As luck would have it, Vasantasena and the Buddhist monk were making their way to Charudatta's house and decided to use the main roads to get there sooner. Vasantasena was very agitated and grew even more so when she saw the huge crowds that had gathered on the road. The executioners were beating their drums and making the final announcement as the crowd swelled and surged. 'What is going on?' cried Vasantasena. What is all this noise?' 'My lady,' said the monk, 'I'm afraid Charudatta is going to be executed for the crime of killing you.' 'We have to stop this!' said Vasantasena, in tears. 'Please, please take me there as fast as you can!' They pushed through the crowd and ran to where Charudatta was being tied up. 'It will be one single stroke, sir,' said the executioner to him. 'We are skilled at our jobs and you will not suffer!' Vasantasena broke through the crowd and threw herself at Charudatta. 'My love, my love!' she cried.

'Vasantasena!' The executioner held back his blow. 'But if you are alive, this man is innocent! Let us go and tell the king what has happened!' 'Wait, wait,' said his partner. 'We were charged with the duty of executing the man who killed Vasantasena. It must be that idiot, the king's brother-in-law. Let's go after him!'

Vasantasena and Charudatta were delirious with joy in each other's arms. The monk broke into their happiness. 'Sir, you should know that I am the man who was engaged as your masseur. I got involved with gamblers and fell into debt, and this kind lady, she paid off what I owed. And now I have given up worldly pleasures and become a monk. Lots of things happened. Your lady got into the wrong carriage and went to the garden where she was attacked by Samsthanaka. He left her there for dead, but then I came along and saved her life.'

In the distance, loud shouts proclaimed Aryaka king. The thief who had stolen Vasantasena's jewels from Charudatta's house was making his way to the execution ground to save Charudatta's life. He was pleasantly surprised to see Charudatta alive and well and in Vasantasena's embrace. 'And who are you?' asked Charudatta as the thief approached them. 'I am the thief who stole the jewels from your house! I have killed wicked Palaka and anointed Aryaka in his place. Aryaka used your carriage to get away from the city.' 'Ah, you must be the clever chap who got Aryaka out of prison,' said Charudatta smiling. 'King Aryaka wants to repay your kindness,' said the thief. 'He has bestowed the kingdom of Kushavati on you and wishes you to reign there for the rest of your years. Now for that scoundrel Samsthanaka. Tie him up and bring him here!' Samsthanaka was dragged out of the crowd and thrown at the thief's feet. The crowd bayed for his blood, shouting, 'Kill him, kill him!' 'What would you like done to him, Charudatta?' said the thief. 'He has wronged you severely.' 'Save me, Charudatta, save me,' blubbered Samsthanaka. 'I'll never do anything to you again.' 'We can behead him, or we can throw him to the dogs,' said the thief, aiming a couple of strong kicks at Samsthanaka's head. 'Let him go free,' said Charudatta. 'Let mercy be his punishment.' Samsthanaka scurried off before he was lynched by the mob.

'Madam, King Aryaka has appointed you Lady of the Court,' said the thief to Vasantasena, who smiled prettily and accepted the honour. 'What does our good monk want?' asked the thief. 'Oh nothing, nothing, all is impermanent, I need nothing,' said the monk modestly. 'Let him be the head of all the monasteries in this region,' said Charudatta. 'And Sthavaraka?' 'Let him go free, let the executioners become chiefs of their guild, let Chandanaka become chief of police,' said Charudatta. 'Vasantasena will be my second wife. All is well! Aryaka is king, you are my friend and our honour has been restored. And we have defeated the wicked by being good. There is nothing more.'

MALATI AND MADHAVA

BY BHAVABHUTI

Best known for his Ramayana masterpiece *Uttararamacarita*, Bhavabhuti was a brahmin who lived and worked in central India in the eighth century CE. Bhavabhuti is admired for his ornate language, complex plots and structures, and *Malatimadhava* is no exception – it has ten acts and a veritable circus of characters playing larger and smaller parts. This, too, is a love story or rather two love stories that intertwine: two couples who are friends inhabit and carry forward the same plot, with their actions impacting the overall narrative of the play.

The saintly Buddhist nun makes an appearance in this play, as she does in other plays in this volume, but Bhavabhuti also gives us a glimpse into non-mainstream practices within Hinduism such as Tantra, for example, and points to the idea that extraordinary powers can be attained by advanced yoga practitioners. We could suggest that, being a follower of more orthodox tradition, Bhavabhuti's depiction of the sorcerer and his apprentice critiques the more extreme practices that had developed in and around Hinduism by the eighth century. Whether or not Bhavabhuti disapproved of these other ways, the modern reader must once again confront the fact that the first millennium of a so-called Hindu past was neither homogeneous nor entirely Hindu.

List of Important Characters

Aghoraghanta – tantric practitioner of black magic
Avalokita – Kamandaki's student
Buddharakshita – attendant
Bhurivasu – father of Malati and minister to the king of Padmavati
Devarata – father of Madhava and minister to the king of Vidarbha
Kalahamsa – Madhava's close friend
Kamandaki – Buddhist nun
Kapalakundala – disciple of the tantric Aghoraghanta
Lavangika – Kamandaki's former student and Malati's friend
Madayantika – Nandana's sister, in love with Makaranda
Madhava – son of Devarata, in love with Malati
Malati – daughter of Bhurivasu, in love with Madhava
Makaranda – Madhava's childhood friend, in love with Madayantika
Mandarika – Malati's attendant, in love with Madhava's friend Kalahamsa
Nandana – Malati's suitor
Saudamini – former student of Kamandaki, now a great yogini

Bhurivasu and Devarata were childhood friends, and in their deep mutual affection, they promised that their yet-unborn children would marry one another. Devarata became a minister to the king of Vidarbha and fathered Madhava, a handsome and intelligent young man who was loved by all. Bhurivasu became a minister to the king of Padmavati, and his daughter, Malati, was the most beautiful young woman in all the land. Devarata sent Madhava to Padmavati to study philosophy, and as he did this, he subtly reminded his friend of their childhood promise. This was also a chance for Madhava to learn the ways of the world and for the people of Padmavati to get to know Madhava and to appreciate his many virtues.

As it happened, there was another man in the city who was interested in the lovely Malati. His name was Nandana and he was a great favourite of the king. Nandana had sent his proposal for Malati's hand to her father, Bhurivasu, through the king himself. Bhurivasu and Devarata kept their plan for their children to themselves – the only person who knew about the promise was Kamandaki, an old Buddhist nun who was Malati's confidante. Kamandaki conspired with Malati's friends to have Madhava frequently walk down the street where Malati lived so that she could see him. She did and was soon enamoured of the handsome young man, so much so that she drew a portrait of him. Her friend Lavangika made sure that the portrait reached Mandarika, who was in love with Kalahamsa, Madhava's attendant. Kamandaki and her student Avalokita plotted further so that the two young people could meet. Since Malati was going to the public gardens to enjoy the celebrations for the God of Love, they made sure that Madhava would be there, too.

As the two women chatted and gossiped, Kamandaki asked about her former student, Saudamini. Avalokita told her that Saudamini had become a powerful yogini and lived in the mountains, practising fierce austerities to augment her powers. Avalokita had heard this from Kapalakundala, another young woman who had become a disciple of the tantric sage Aghoraghanta, who lived in the cremation ground and worshipped the bloodthirsty goddess Chamunda. 'Enough of this, let's go to the garden and find Malati,' said Avalokita. Along the way, she said to Kamandaki, 'Wouldn't it be wonderful if we could arrange a marriage between Makaranda, Madhava's childhood friend, and Nandana's sister Madayantika? It would make Madhava very happy if his friend made a good marriage alliance.'

Many of the city's young people were making their way to the public gardens, excited to participate in the celebrations. Makaranda saw his beloved friend, Madhava, coming towards him. But Madhava was wan and pale and seemed distracted, lost in his thoughts, muttering to himself as he walked along. Makaranda greeted him and led him to a shady bench where they could sit and talk. 'You seem to be returning from the celebrations in the garden, so why do you look so downcast? Could it be that you have been struck by the arrows of the God of Love?' he asked playfully. Madhava heaved a burning sigh. 'Let me tell you what happened. I went to the garden and sat down in the shade of a bakula tree, laden with flowers and heavy with their perfume. I was so overcome by the fragrance that I began to gather the flowers and string them together in a garland. And then I saw this exquisite woman emerge from the temple of the God of Love, surrounded by her attendants. She was a veritable treasure house of beauty, her skin like the moon, her every feature a wonder in itself. Her maids brought her to sit under the same tree and gathered flowers for her. When that gorgeous creature came closer, I could see that she was in love – she was listless, her movements were languid, and she sighed heavily every now and then. My heart was drawn to her like iron to a magnet. There was nothing I could do. I was helpless. But her companions acted as if they knew me – they looked at me from under their eyelashes and they laughed and giggled, making sweet music with their jingling bracelets and ankle bells. And then that lovely woman looked over at me and seemed to swoon, displaying all the signs of love. I could barely contain my agitation when she was led away by her companions and rode back to the city on a magnificent elephant.'

'And who is this lady? Did you find out who she was?' Makaranda was eager to know more. Madhava continued: 'When she was leaving, I gave the flower garland I had made to one of her friends. She took it from me and thanked me, and I felt as if her glances were full of meaning, as if she was trying to tell me something. I asked her who her mistress was and she told me that she was Malati, daughter of our minister Bhurivasu.' Makaranda said to himself, 'Ah, yes. Kamandaki speaks very highly of her. I believe that Nandana also has an interest in her and that the king himself has sent a proposal on Nandana's behalf.' To his friend, he said, 'This is happy news, Malati has shown her love for you. All that languor and paleness indicates that her feelings are quite strong. But where has she seen you before for her love to be so intense?' Kalahamsa, who had been eavesdropping on their conversation, stepped out from where he had concealed himself and produced the portrait of Madhava that Malati had drawn. 'The very lady that you love made this portrait to ease her longing for you!' he said triumphantly. 'Friend, take strength from the fact that the object of your affections has feelings for you, too!' said Makaranda. 'We would like to see her beauty, too. Why don't you make a portrait of her?' Kalahamsa produced a board and some paints, and from memory, Madhava drew a picture of the woman he had just seen.

Mandarika, one of Malati's attendants, came to where the friends were, having followed Kalahamsa, the man she loved. When they showed her the portrait of Malati, she was surprised. 'Where did you get this from? Who made it?' she asked. 'It was made by the very person in Malati's portrait,' said Kalahamsa. 'But where did Malati see Madhava?' asked Makaranda. 'From the window when he used to walk on our street,' replied Mandarika. 'Now, give this to me and I will make sure that it reaches my mistress through Lavangika! And I'll also make sure that she knows who drew it!'

Lavangika and Malati were sitting on the terrace, talking about the events of the day. When Lavangika gave Malati the garland of flowers that Madhava had given her, Malati was overcome with emotion, fretting about whether Madhava's gestures had been a game or whether he truly loved her. Lavangika then gave her the portrait that Madhava had made, saying that surely Madhava reciprocated her love. The young women continued to whisper and laugh and talk about love. Kamandaki, who had already heard about the events of the morning, was pleased that her plans for the young people were working out smoothly.

Meanwhile, the king had made the demand that everyone dreaded – he had asked for Malati's hand in marriage for his dear friend Nandana. Bhurivasu's response to this offer for his daughter's hand had been ambiguous. He had said, 'Let Your Majesty dispose of Your Majesty's daughter as Your Majesty pleases.' Malati was distraught when she heard the news and lamented that her father loved the king more than he loved her. Madhava, too, was deeply unhappy and promptly fell ill. Kamandaki came to visit Malati and subtly turned her mind against her father and against her new fiancé. At the same time, she heaped praises on Madhava. She told Malati about the promise her father had made to Madhava's father when they were young and that Madhava was not simply the most suitable partner for her but that their fathers had vowed they would be together. Malati was cheered by these revelations and Kamandaki left, her mind full of further plans to unite the two young lovers.

Kamandaki sent Madhava a message that he should go to the Shiva temple on the last day of the dark half of the month and that Malati would be there to meet him. At the same time, Malati's friends told her that this was an auspicious night to worship Shiva with flowers that she had gathered herself and to ask for his favour. Meanwhile, there was another love story unfolding on the side. A young woman named Madayantika, Nandana's sister, was in love with Makaranda. They, too, were to meet each other at the same Shiva temple on the same night.

Kamandaki also went to the Shiva temple on the appointed night. Soon, Malati arrived with Lavangika, and all three went to the kadamba tree to gather flowers for Malati's ritual. Madhava was already there, and he noticed that Malati was looking care-worn and tired, but his own heart rose and fluttered with joy when he saw her. Kamandaki and the two young women sat down together and Kamandaki began to tell Malati all about Madhava – how noble he was and how he had been struck down by a fever when he heard that Malati had been promised to Nandana as a bride. Lavangika recounted how Malati, too, was not herself, how she wore the garland that Madhava had made all the time. Lavangika wondered how long the lovers would be able to bear their separation.

Unexpectedly, a voice came from the distance. 'Beware, all who are in the temple garden! A massive tiger has escaped – a young beast, strong and powerful. He broke through his cage and terrified men and animals as he rampaged through the grounds. His trail is bloody with those that he has killed and injured and his roar is terrifying. Beware, Beware!' At the same time, an attendant shouted, 'Help me, help me! My friend Madayantika is being attacked by the tiger – her friends have all been killed!' Madhava, worried for his friend Makaranda, jumped up from where he had been hiding and ran off to help. He noticed that Malati's face had brightened when she saw him and that gave him a renewed vigour. But brave Makaranda had already faced down the tiger. There had been a terrible fight between man and beast until, at last, the tiger lay slain and Makaranda stood, leaning on his sword, reeling and faint from the loss of blood. Both Madayantika and Makaranda were brought to Kamandaki, who revived them and dressed their wounds.

Madayantika recognized Makaranda from all that she had heard about him. Moreover, she was in his debt for having saved her life, and that feeling of gratitude changed quickly into a deeper attraction. Kamandaki noticed the shy glances that Madayantika and Makaranda had exchanged and was pleased that another worthy young couple had fallen in love. Malati and Madhava, too, were enjoying their own reunion. Madhava told Kamandaki that the sight of Malati had brought him back from the abyss of despair. 'As a token of my thanks, I offer Malati both my heart and my life!' he said happily.

But their joy was not to last long as news came announcing the date for the marriage ceremony between Malati and Nandana. Madayantika, who was the bridegroom's sister, was thrilled, for she had known and loved Malati since they had played together as children. But Malati and Madhava were stricken, unable to believe what had happened to them. Kamandaki spoke to Madhava. 'Listen to me. Don't give up. Bhurivasu's words could mean that the king has power over his own daughter, not that the king may give away the daughter of another person. This means that it is still incumbent on me to bring you two together, even if it's at the cost of my life!' 'Good lady, your affection for these young people, your children, goes against the fundamental principles of renunciation,' said Makaranda with admiration. 'That, too, must be fate!' The queen called Kamandaki away and told her to bring Malati with her. Malati and Madhava, certain in their hearts that this was the last time they would be together, could not tear their eyes away from each other.

Madhava saw the life he had dreamed of vanish as Malati walked away. He was overcome with despair and in his mind, the only solution he could think of was to seek the help of dark forces and magic. He decided to seek favour from the goddess Chamunda and her devotees by selling them the human flesh they needed for their rituals. The flesh he sold them was strips cut from his own body. He kept his courage up by remembering his love for Malati and recalling her beauty, limb by limb. One night, as he sat in the cremation ground, surrounded by funeral pyres that lit up heaps of skulls and bones and, as the dense and acrid smoke of burning flesh rose around him, he noticed a great commotion. Ghouls, goblins and flesh-eating ghosts were emerging from dark corners and trees. Tantric sages and sadhus were arriving on foot and through the air. Creatures of the night were feasting and dancing, their lips red with blood, their bodies covered with ash and adorned with skulls and bones for, on this night, Aghoraghanta, the tantric master, was going to sacrifice a beautiful young virgin to the goddess.

Above the shrieks and growls and snarls and screams in the cremation ground, Madhava heard a human voice. 'Oh, cruel father! This body with which you sought to please the king is going to be destroyed!' Madhava followed the voice, which was clearly that of a woman in distress, and came to the temple of Chamunda. Inside, he saw Aghoraghanta and his female assistant, Kapalakundala, dressed in their ceremonial attire, ready to perform their ghastly ritual. To his horror, their victim was none other than his beloved Malati. She was calling out to her parents and friends in a piteous voice. 'Oh, mother, father, dear Kamandaki, sweet Lavangika! You shall never see me again, remember me fondly . . . !' Aghoraghanta and his ghoulish followers danced in a frenzy, bowing to the goddess, singing her praises and asking for her favour. 'Think as much as you like about the people you love, death is very close!' cackled Kapalakundala. Aghoraghanta drew his sword and shouted, 'I don't care whom she loves. It is time to kill her! We can delay no longer, the auspicious moment has arrived!'

Just as he was about to cut off Malati's head, Madhava rushed in and snatched up his beloved. 'Who is this fool who interrupts our sacred ritual!' Aghoraghanta screamed in rage. 'How did you get here?' Madhava asked Malati as they fled. 'I don't know,' she said through her tears. 'All I remember is that I was asleep on the terrace and when I awoke, I was in this terrible place! But what about you, what are you doing here?' Madhava told her that since he could not bear life without her, he had come to the cremation ground to befriend the dark forces that would bring her back to him. Aghoraghanta had followed them. 'Stop, you brahmin dog!' he shouted. 'I will make the goddess happy by letting your blood flow freely on the temple floor when I have chopped off your head!'

Just then a voice called out from behind the temple: 'Soldiers who are in search of Malati, listen to me! Surround this temple! Aghoraghanta is the one who has planned this human sacrifice, and Malati, the daughter of our minister Bhurivasu is his victim!' Kapalakundala shrieked, 'Master, master, we are surrounded!' Madhava dodged the ghouls and goblins that had gathered and sped away with Malati, setting her down safely among the soldiers who had surrounded the temple to rescue her. Then he ran back into the temple and attacked Aghoraghanta and, after a bitter and bloody fight, Madhava slew him. From the shadows of that dark place on that dark night, Kapalakundala watched and swore that she would avenge the death of her master.

Soon after, preparations were being made for Malati's wedding to Madhava in the city. Madhava was terribly upset, but Makaranda and Kalahamsa persuaded him to watch Malati's magnificent wedding procession. 'Don't give up hope,' said Makaranda. 'This is just the procession, she's not married yet. Keep your faith in Kamandaki, she will not let you down!' The wedding procession went by, and the friends left the balcony from which they were watching.

Kamandika and Lavangika were with Malati, who said nothing but wished for death to take her away and put an end to her misery. A female attendant arrived carrying the bridal garments for Malati to wear. Kamandika took them, smiling, and told Lavangika to take Malati inside the temple while she herself examined the jewels and the other wedding finery. Unbeknownst to Malati, Madhava and Makaranda were already hiding in the temple. Lavangika showed Malati the perfumed oils and the flower garlands that had arrived for her, but Malati pushed them aside and said, 'Dear friend, these are of no interest to me. I am about to die, unwed. But I want you to hold me in your heart forever. Tell Madhava that if my love has meant anything at all, he should not forget me.'

Madhava's joy knew no bounds as he listened to Malati confessing her undying love for him, but instead of revealing himself, he waited patiently. 'I will not listen to such awful words anymore!' cried Lavangika. 'Dear friend,' said Malati sadly. 'I have lived my life in the false hope that I would marry the man I love. Those days are gone, I want to die now, still innocent of having betrayed him, whom I love most. Do not deny me that!' Sobbing, Malati fell to the ground. Lavangika bent to lift her up and signalled to Madhava to come out from behind the pillar and take her place.

Madhava stepped in and when Malati begged Lavangika to release her from this life, Madhava said, 'But I could never live without you!' 'I will not move until you let me die!' said Malati, who was so upset that she was oblivious to who was lifting her. 'Well then, so shall it be,' said Madhava. 'But first, let us embrace.' Malati cried even more and said, 'My eyes are so dim from crying, I cannot see very well. I know I will live forever in your memory. Thank you for making that possible. And I want to give you this memento from Madhava . . . '

Malati took the garland that Madhava had made for her from her neck and placed it around the neck of the person who was holding her. She fell back when she realized who it was. 'Lavangika, you have betrayed me!' she wept. Madhava spoke to her gently. 'You think only of all that you have endured in our separation. Think of me, too. I was incapacitated by fever, I could do nothing, neither think nor breathe. It was only the promise of our love that kept me alive!' Makaranda spoke up in his friend's defence. 'Dear lady, this man has suffered for you. Now, all we need is the golden thread that will bind you in marriage.' Kamandaki entered the temple, and Malati threw herself into the old woman's arms. 'Come my child,' Kamandaki said sweetly. 'This man is your first and only love, the one who stole your heart. Accept him, and let the wishes of the God of Love be fulfilled!' She blessed the young couple, both of whom meant so much to her.

Meanwhile, Makaranda had disappeared with the bridal garments. He emerged from the inner room of the temple, fully dressed, laughing, 'Behold! I am now Malati!' Madhava joined in the laughter. 'Lucky Nandana, to get a bride like this!' 'Come now, children,' said Kamandaki. 'Go to the garden behind my house.

Avalokita is there and has made all the arrangements for a simple wedding ceremony. Wait there for Makaranda and Madayantika. Come, Lavangika, we need to be somewhere else!'

Sometime later, Makaranda (as Malati) and Lavangika were sitting together. They heard the tinkling of Madayantika's anklets, and quickly, Lavangika covered Makaranda with a blanket. 'Pretend to be asleep,' she whispered. Lavangika hushed Madayantika, saying that Malati was exhausted from the night before and had just fallen asleep. 'I heard that she has been very rude and badly behaved with my brother, her new husband,' said Madayantika. 'He was violent towards her and said the most terrible things,' retorted Lavangika. 'He said that he wanted nothing more to do with such a wanton woman! Such rudeness cannot be condoned.' 'Oh, I do not condone those words,' said Madayantika, tartly. 'But he had cause to say them. The whole city knows that Malati had first given her heart to Madhava. Besides, when that gallant man rescued me from the tiger, I heard Madhava say that he had given his heart to Malati and you yourself accepted it on her behalf! Do you remember that young man who saved my life?' Lavangika took her time to respond and then said, 'Ah, yes. That was Makaranda. What is he to you?' 'Nothing,' said Madayantika, blushing. Then she lowered her voice. 'I have erotic dreams about him. And when I wake, the whole world is bland and colourless!' Lavangika suppressed a giggle. 'What would you do if you were to see Makaranda again?' she asked. 'I would let my eyes feast slowly on each of his limbs and savour the sight, as slowly as possible!' said Madayantika. Lavangika went further: 'And what if he were to make off with you as a bride, the way Krishna took Subhadra?' 'Why do you torment me with hopes like this?' Madayantika sighed. They heard bells toll for the second watch of the night.

As Madayantika prepared to leave, Makaranda grabbed her hand. 'Ah, Malati,' said Madayantika. 'You are awake?' Makaranda revealed himself, and quickly, Lavangika said, 'Come, come, let us leave at once. The night is dark and the servants are asleep!' 'Where are you taking me?' Madayantika asked. 'To where Malati is!' replied Lavangika.

Madhava and Malati were enjoying each other's company on that cool summer night, sitting outdoors under the moon. Avalokita joined them, and they chatted about this and that. Avalokita teased Madhava: 'You have already pledged your life and your heart to Malati. What gift do you have left to give her, should the occasion arise?' 'I have this garland of bakula flowers which I made the first time I saw Malati in the garden. I sent it to her then, but in the anxiety around her wedding ceremony, she gave it to me, mistaking me for Lavangika.' 'Be careful, then,' said Avalokita, 'that it doesn't fall into the wrong hands!' 'Good news! Madayantika has been won over by Makaranda,' said Malati. 'I am so happy!' said Madhava and placed the bakula garland around her neck.

But their happiness was disturbed by Kalahamsa, who came rushing in with Lavangika, Madayantika and Buddharakshita. 'Makaranda was attacked by the city guards on our way,' cried Lavangika. 'We ran here with Kalahamsa, but we could hear shouting behind us. The guards are probably getting reinforcements. You must rescue Makaranda!' 'Don't worry, Makaranda is the best fighter I know. He will be able to take care of himself until Kalahamsa and I join him!' said Madhava as he and Kalahamsa left in haste. After a while, Malati sent Avalokita and Buddharakshita to tell Kamandaki what had happened and she sent Lavangika off to get news of the skirmish with the city guards. But as time passed, she began to get restless and fretful, wondering why Lavangika had not returned. All of a sudden, Kapalakundala swooped down from the sky and grabbed Malati, who screamed for Madhava. 'Yes, yes,' mocked Kapalakundala. 'Ask that husband of yours for help. He's no use to you. I'm going to take you to the top of the mountain and cut you up into little pieces and give you a truly agonising death!'

Madhava and Makaranda came back, flushed with their victory over the guards and pleased that the king had noticed them and praised them. The king had also reprimanded both Devarata and Bhurivasu, saying that they should be proud to have such fine young men as their sons-in-law. Madayantika fell into Makaranda's arms, and Madhava said, 'Come now, tell us everything about how Madayantika was taken. I want to hear this story along with Malati. Where is Malati?' They searched for her everywhere but with no luck. Madhava began to worry, convinced that something bad had happened and that his beloved was in danger. Unable to find Malati anywhere in the city, Madhava started to look in the mountains for her. His faithful friend Makaranda went with him, and it was all that he could do to keep Madhava's spirits up as the days without news or sight of Malati grew longer and more desperate. Madhava floated in and out of reality and delusions and Makaranda began to lose hope of his friend ever regaining his mind. Rather than live without Madhava, Makaranda decided to commit suicide by throwing himself into the river.

Out of nowhere, Saudamini, Kamandaki's former student, who had become a powerful yogini, appeared and stopped him. 'Are you not Makaranda?' she said. 'Look, I have a memento from Malati!' She held out the bakula garland and said, 'Let us go at once to broken-hearted Madhava and give him a reason to live!' When Saudamini dropped the garland into Madhava's lap, he recognized it at once and pressed it to his heart. Saudamini appeared and confirmed Madhava's worst fear – Malati was alive but had been abducted by Kapalakundala in revenge for the killing of Aghoraghanta. Saudamini promised Madhava that she would use all her powers to rescue Malati. She took him away, leaving Makaranda open-mouthed with wonder on the mountain slopes.

Kamandaki, Madayantika and Lavangika had also made their way to the mountain and were ready to throw themselves into the deep valleys between the peaks. They could not bear the loss of their beloved friend and had convinced themselves that she was dead. Suddenly, out of the clear blue sky, there was a great flash, like lightning, and a huge sound reverberated around the mountain.

Kamandaki was the first to react. 'What is this? Who is there?' she asked. Makaranda joined them and said, 'This can only mean one thing. The great yogini has arrived!' In the distance, a crowd was gathering. They heard people shouting, 'Bhurivasu is so depressed at the loss of his daughter that he is coming to this mountain to throw himself into a fire!' Kamandaki said, 'What a day this is that alternates between darkness and light, between joy and sorrow, between the sharp blades of swords and the sweetness of sandalwood!' Then, they heard Malati's voice. 'O father, wait! Don't do this! Let me see you again! Turn your face to me and look upon me, your daughter!' 'What is this new calamity?' cried Kamandaki. 'Dear Malati, you had just been rescued. Why is your life in danger again!'

Madhava appeared, carrying an almost lifeless Malati in his arms. 'She nearly died of suffocation,' he said, 'she was just recovering, but then she heard the terrible news about her father, and now she is unable to breathe. It seems as if life is leaving her body!' 'Let us call upon the great yogini – she is the only one who can save us!' the others called out to the yogini in panic and in grief, wailing and crying and beating their breasts. A stream of cool water, fresh and sparkling, poured down from that same clear sky as if there had been a cloudburst. 'She's alive, she's alive!' shouted Madhava. 'She's breathing, and I can feel her heartbeat!' In the distance, they heard a voice announce that Bhurivasu had stepped back from the flames. Malati recovered and was joyfully greeted by all her friends and her family.

The great yogini Saudamini appeared, and everyone fell at her feet, thanking her and praising her. Malati said, 'She rescued me from that awful creature Kapalakundala and took me to her place and kept me safe. Then she took the garland of bakula flowers for Madhava and roused him from his despair.' Saudamini laughed. 'I am oppressed by these thanks,' she said. 'They stifle me. But here is a letter from the king. Dear teacher, read it to us all.' Kamandaki took the letter and said, 'The king wants us to know that he is pleased to have Madhava, first in merit and courage, as his son-in-law and equally pleased to bestow upon his worthy comrade, Makaranda, the well-born and lovely Madayantika.'

'I could not be happier,' said Madhava. 'Every wish of mine has been fulfilled.' More rejoicing and celebrations broke out among the group of friends. Avalokita and Buddharakshita had also joined the party, as had Kalahamsa. 'This has all worked out even better than expected because an old promise has been kept!' said Saudamini. 'What promise?' they all asked. Kamandaki explained. 'The fathers of our loving couple, Malati and Madhava, had betrothed their children to each other long ago. Fate and Saudamini ensured that even that vow was upheld! This is truly a happy ending to all our troubles!'

YAUGANDHARAYANA'S VOW

BY BHASA

It is likely that Bhasa lived in the first or second century CE, closer in time to the Buddhist philosopher and playwright Ashvaghosha than to Kalidasa. Kalidasa was the playwright who wrote plays that perfectly matched the requirements of Sanskrit dramaturgy and aesthetics, and Bhasa, about whom we know very little, was the outlier in this universe. Although his works are mentioned in other classical Sanskrit texts, Bhasa's plays, thirteen in all, were rediscovered as recently as 1913.

Bhasa is best known for his Mahabharata plays, but here, in *Pratijna Yaugandharayana*, he turns to another great story text, the *Brihatkatha,* for inspiration and finds the long narrative of King Udayana and his faithful and clever minister, Yaugandharayana, who not only helps the king win his beloved but also negotiates an alliance with a powerful local monarch. Although the plot of the play involves what can only be called a Trojan elephant and has as its climax an elephant chase, this is one among few Sanskrit plays that does more for its actors than for its story. Yaugandharayana and his trusty comrades spend half the play in disguise, one as a beggar, one as a madman and one as a Buddhist monk. There are also reassuring flashes of realism that we can relate to, as in the brief conversations between King Mahasena and his wife as they discuss the marriage prospects of their daughter, who is preparing to elope with Udayana.

List of Important Characters

Badarayana – Mahasena's chamberlain
Bharatarohaka – Mahasena's prime minister
Hamsaka – attendant
Mahasena – king of Avanti
Queen – Mahasena's wife
Queen Mother – Udayana's mother
Udayana – king of Vatsa
Vasavadatta – princess of Avanti
Yaugandharayana, Vasantaka, Rumanvat – Udayana's ministers

PROLOGUE

Before the play opens, King Udayana's story has already begun. When he was born, a voice came out of the sky predicting that he would be a glorious king. His mother had birthed him in the hermitage of the great sage Jamadagni, who became the boy's teacher. Udayana grew up playing with forest animals and enjoying the pleasures of climbing trees and swimming in lakes and streams.

One day, he saw a man capturing a snake. Udayana asked him to free the snake, but the man replied saying he made his living by selling snakes. Udayana immediately took off the bracelet his mother had given him and offered it to the man as a price for the snake, which the man accepted. The snake was Vasunemi, brother of Vasuki, the mighty king of the snakes. In gratitude, Vasunemi gave Udayana an enchanted sitar that could create the most exquisite music and taught him how to play it. He also gave Udayana a magic formula that would ensure that his wife's betel leaves were always green and tender, that the flower garlands she strung would always remain fresh and that the vermillion streak she put on her forehead would never fade.

In time, Udayana left the hermitage and was united with his father, who was overjoyed to have such a fine son. He anointed him crown prince and gave him Vasantaka, Rumanvat and Yaugandharayana, sons of his own ministers, as companions and advisors. When the king retired to the forest, Udayana happily took over his duties and ruled the kingdom of Vatsa for some years. But after a while, he handed over the kingdom to his ministers and began to spend more and more time hunting wild elephants that he lured into his presence by playing his sitar. He seemed to have only one anxiety: that there was no one good enough for him to marry except Princess Vasavadatta, the daughter of a powerful neighbouring king, Pradyota Mahasena of Avanti. Mahasena had his eye on Udayana as a prospective son-in-law and set about making plans for this alliance. He decided that he would capture Udayana and bring him to Ujjain, his capital city. Once Udayana was there, Mahasena would send Vasavadatta to him to learn how to play the sitar. He was sure that Udayana would fall in love with his daughter, which would make the marriage and the political alliance a simple matter.

Mahasena's ministers suggested that it would be better to put the same plan in motion through diplomacy rather than aggression and so, Mahasena sent Udayana a formal invitation to come to Ujjain to teach his daughter music. Udayana laughed at the insulting prospect of a king being asked to go to another kingdom as a music teacher and turned down the offer. Mahasena had no choice now but to bring Udayana to Ujjain by force. He constructed an elephant that looked just like his own royal mount. An entire battalion of warriors was hidden inside the elephant, which was then installed in the forests that lay between the two kingdoms.

Yaugandharayana had found out about Mahasena's ploy with the artificial elephant and the hidden warriors. As he was making his own plans to ensure Udayana stayed away from those forests, he received a message that Udayana had already left on his usual hunting trip. Shortly after that, he was told that Hamsaka, an attendant who never left Udayana's side, had come to see him and that he was alone.

Yaugandharayana grew worried and questioned Hamsaka anxiously, only to learn that Udayana had been captured by Mahasena's men. 'But why was the king alone in the forest? Where was his usual armed escort?' Hamasaka said, 'The king was on a picnic with the royal ladies and one morning, at dawn, he set off for the elephant forests with a small force, just enough to deal with a herd of elephants. He took a narrow path, more suitable for deer and other small animals. Once we got to the forest, we saw a herd of elephants about a mile away, playing in a stream. A foot soldier appeared from nowhere . . . ' Yaugandharayana interrupted, 'Did he tell you that he had seen a blue elephant covered with jasmine creepers and hidden by sala trees?' 'How did you know that?' Hamsaka asked in surprise. 'Anyway, our king gave the man a hundred pieces of gold and said that this was probably the emperor elephant and that he was determined to enchant him with music.

Minister Rumanvat tried to stop him by warning him that the forest people in the area were quite aggressive and that he should not go alone. But the king made the minister swear an oath not to interfere and rode off on his horse with only twenty men. By then, we had realized that the elephant was a fake, but the hidden warriors had already emerged from it, and though our king fought as hard and bravely as he could, he was soon overpowered and he fainted. And the worst is yet to come – those uncouth men tied him up like a common criminal with ropes made from forest vines and creepers.

But fortunately, one of King Mahasena's officers appeared and forbade any further violence. He bowed to our king and set him free. And when he noticed our king was too weak to walk, he had him placed in a litter and taken away.' Yaugandharayana groaned. 'This exceeds Mahasena's expectations by far – our king has been humiliated. I don't know how he will bear his captivity.' He turned to the doorkeeper and said, 'Go and tell the queen mother what has happened. But do it gently, for a mother's heart is a fragile thing. Start by talking about the dangers of war, talk about cruel and sharp weapons. When she prepares for the worst by thinking that her son has been killed, let her know that he is alive but a prisoner.' The doorkeeper left to deliver the news.

'But what are you doing here? Why are you not with the king?' Yaugandharayana asked Hamsaka. 'I was sent here with the news,' he replied. 'Did the king mention me?' Yaugandharayana was anxious to know. 'Yes, he did,' Hamsaka said. 'And anyone else by name? The ministers? The Council?' Yaugandharayana had a sinking feeling. 'No, sir,' Hamsaka answered briefly. 'Then he is disappointed in me,' said Yaugandharayana. 'I did not take enough precautions, I have not proved my loyalty, I have not earned my keep. I shall change! I shall prove to the king that I am worthy of him! Wherever he is, I will be devoted to him. I will defeat King Mahasena who thinks he is victorious! My master shall soon have reason to praise his loyal servant!'

The sound of women weeping and wailing drifted into the room when the doorkeeper returned. She had brought a message from the queen mother which said: 'This has happened even to someone as brave and courageous as the king of Vatsa who is surrounded by friends and well-wishers. There is nothing we can do to divert fate and so now, we must turn to his friends and take heart. There is one man here, he is like a son to me – he is wise and does not falter in the face of misfortune or lose hope when all seems lost. I beseech this man, as a minister and a friend of the king, to bring my son back to me!'

Yaugandharayana asked for some water and took a sip. Then he spoke with great resolve. 'I shall liberate our king who has been taken by force, like the moon taken by the demon of the eclipse!' Just then, another attendant entered. 'Sir,' he said, 'the local brahmins were going to a feast after the performance of auspicious rituals for the king's safety. There appeared among them another brahmin, dressed like a madman, who said, "Eat, eat, eat all you can, for this kingdom is soon to be blessed with great prosperity!" And then, he disappeared.' A brahmin came into the room and said, 'Here are the peculiar clothes he was wearing. I am sure it was the great Vyasa himself who was among us.' Yaugandharayana's face lit up. 'These clothes have been left for me as inspiration. They will take me into our king's presence and will help me set him free! Rubbing a stick against another produces fire, digging the earth produces water – nothing is impossible for those who dare!'

In Ujjain, King Mahasena's city, there was a steady stream of envoys from neighbouring kingdoms, all asking for the hand of Vasavadatta in marriage. Mahasena treated them all well, showering them with the best hospitality, but he showed favour to none. It was clear he was waiting for a proposal from one king in particular.

He came into his court one morning, followed by the entire royal entourage and called for his chamberlain. He muttered to himself, 'Kings from far and near accept my authority. But I shall not be satisfied until that one king from Vatsa, so arrogant and proud of his facility with elephants, bows his head before me.' When the chamberlain, Badarayana, entered, the king complimented him on all the fine arrangements he had made to look after the visitors from other royal courts. 'No one tells me what they really think when I talk about the princess's betrothal. You tell me, Badarayana, what do you think?' 'No one says anything because, although you do not turn anyone away, you also do not seem interested in anyone. Why is that?' asked the chamberlain. 'Well, you know that I want only the very best for my daughter because I am so very fond of her. The man must have a fine and noble lineage, but he must also be tender-hearted, for that is a great virtue. Of course, he must be handsome and strong and brave.' 'There is no one like that in the world except you, Majesty!' the chamberlain smiled. 'This is the most important task for a father, finding a suitable mate for his daughter. But send for the queen. I know that mothers' hearts break when their daughters are given away in marriage.'

When the queen arrived, King Mahasena asked fondly after his daughter and was told that she had decided to take music lessons and was looking for a suitable teacher. 'Why does she need a teacher here when she'll be married soon? Let her husband teach her!' retorted the king. The queen's eyes filled with tears at the thought that she would soon be separated from her daughter. The king noticed and began to tell her about the many proposals that had come for Vasavadatta. He told her who the kings were and about their various talents and virtues. He also mentioned that he had not made up his mind and asked his queen who she thought might be worthy. 'The king of Vatsa!' interrupted the chamberlain. The king and queen both turned around in surprise. 'Pardon me, Sire! I was so happy to give you the good news that I broke protocol,' Badarayana said. 'What is this good news, then?' asked the king. 'Our minister has captured Udayana, king of Vatsa!' said Badarayana, triumphantly. 'Is Yaugandharayana dead?' said the king. 'Udayana could not have been taken otherwise – we all know how brave Yaugandharayana is and what a clever strategist. Are you sure this is true?' 'I am too old to lie, Your Majesty,' said the chamberlain. 'Our minister is on his way here with Udayana!' 'Well then,' said the king, 'we shall not have our daughter engaged to anyone at the moment.'

The queen said, 'My lord, I have never seen you in such a state of excitement before!' 'I have never had an occasion to be this excited before!' laughed the king. 'I want all my people to see this man, this king, caged like a lion!' 'Why has his family not sent us an offer of marriage for our daughter?' asked the queen. 'He ignores me, this Vatsa,' said the king. 'Why? Is he a boy? Or a fool?' the queen asked petulantly. 'Neither,' said the king. 'He is proud of his lineage and his dynasty, who have ruled these northern plains for centuries. They are learned, and they are all wonderful musicians.

He is good-looking and his people love him – all this makes him confident,' said the king. The chamberlain walked in carrying a sitar. 'The honourable minister offers you this as a gift, the legendary Ghoshavati that was always played in the Vatsa family. They say when it is played by a skilled performer, the instrument can tame even rutting elephants.' 'I shall take this as a symbol of victory,' Mahasena said. He could not have been more pleased. 'Now, who should I give this to? Lady, did you not say that our daughter had suddenly developed an interest in music? Let her have it. It will encourage her to play better. Tell me, Badarayana, where is Udayana?' 'He has been so badly wounded that he was brought to the palace on a stretcher,' replied Badarayana. 'That's what happens when you insist on being brave,' muttered the king. 'See to it that he is well taken care of, his every wound treated and dressed. He must be comfortable at all times. You must anticipate his wishes and meet all his needs. Do not speak of war, and bless him every time he sneezes. Make sure that he is given a room inside the palace to recover, away from the sun.' 'So,' said the queen archly, 'have we chosen a bridegroom for our little girl?' 'Not quite yet,' said the king softly. To himself, he thought, 'I used to hate him for his haughty pride. And when they brought him here, I was almost neutral. But now, when I hear about his condition, his life in danger – I don't know how to think about my feelings for him any more.'

Meanwhile, Udayana's companions had reached Ujjain, travelling separately, in their bid to rescue him. Vasantaka, the brahmin, was in disguise as a beggar and was hanging about near the Shiva temple. He had brought a bowl of sweets to offer to the deity and was making a great commotion about having placed his offering somewhere and now being unable to find it. A madman, who was, of course, Yaugandharayana, wandered in, carrying a bowl of sweets and offering them to anyone who would take them. Vasantaka and Yaugandharayana began to argue about who the sweets belonged to, identifying each other through various codes and puns, when a Buddhist monk appeared. The madman offered him the sweets and the monk promptly spat on them. 'Stay away from these,' he exhorted the other two. 'They are not good for you!' The madman started walking in the direction of one of the smaller shrines and the other two followed him, still squabbling about who should have the sweets. In that deserted place, the trio laughed and embraced each other.

Yaugandharayana asked Vasantaka if he had been able to see Udayana. 'I have, indeed,' Vasantaka said proudly. 'Today is the fourteenth day and I was able to attend to him at his bath and worship the gods, at least a little.' 'Go to him again tonight,' said Yaugandharayana, 'and tell him of our plan. I have arranged for the king's elephant, Nalagiri, to be provoked. We have placed herbs that disturb elephants close to where he eats and sleeps. There will be smoke that will blow towards him when the wind rises. The elephant opposite him is in rut. An empty building near the stable will be set on fire – you know that elephants are afraid of fire. With all this chaos and Nalagiri's distress, King Mahasena is sure to call on our king to manage the situation. Our king will be let out of prison by the very man who captured him! He will have his sitar, he will climb onto Nalagiri's back and flee. No one will be able to catch him. He will reach Vatsa safely. He was lured here, to Avanti, by an elephant, albeit a fake one, and he will escape on a real one!'

'I fear this plan will not work,' said Vasantaka. 'Let me tell you what has happened. A week ago, Princess Vasavadatta went to worship at the shrine opposite the prison. Being a young girl, she was in an open palanquin. Our dear king, on that very day, had permission from a prison officer to spend some time outside the prison and he saw the princess at close quarters.' 'Surely he has not fallen in love with her,' cried Yaugandharayana. 'Indeed he has!' said Vasantaka rather jauntily. 'He also said to tell you that he does not like your plan about escaping right away. I want to do something that really insults Mahasena as I leave, the king said. "This will avenge the way he has humiliated me!" I think we have proved our devotion and done the best we can. We should leave him where he is and go back home,' Vasantaka concluded.

Yaugandharayana could not believe his ears. 'Shame on you, Vasantaka,' he said. 'Can this really be you speaking?' 'We could be in this situation till we are old and grey!' retorted Vasantaka. 'If you want to rescue him in the way he wants, you will have to get him out of prison and get the princess out of the palace.' 'Here is my second vow,' said Yaugandharayana firmly. 'I will make sure that our king escapes with the princess, as Arjuna did with Subhadra. And I will be the one to take both of them to safety!' Rumanvat cautioned his friends, 'I can hear people enjoying the evening air and gathering here in the temple complex. There are four doors to this shrine. Let us disperse and keep ourselves safe!'

Sometime later, a soldier went looking for the mahout who took care of Bhadravati, Princess Vasavadatta's gentle elephant. He found him staggering about, quite drunk. 'Hey, you!' said the soldier. 'The princess wants to go bathing and cannot find her elephant. And here you are, drunk! Go, bring the elephant right this minute!' 'Oh, I can't do that,' slurred the mahout. 'I pawned her goad.' 'You don't need the goad, Bhadravati is so gentle,' countered the soldier. 'Well, I sold her beautiful necklace, too.' 'Adorn her with flowers and bring her along. She doesn't need a necklace,' said the soldier. As they bickered back and forth, there was a cry from the highway, 'King Udayana of Vatsa has taken Princess Vasavadatta and departed!' 'May he face no obstacles!' said the mahout happily. 'All of us here are Yaugandharayana's spies. I simply have to signal my friends. Woe to the man who will not fight for his master and earn the food that he eats.' The mahout saw that a fierce battle was raging on the highway. Yaugandharayana had given up his disguise as a madman and was in the thick of things, fighting with both sword and spear, giving as good as he got. But he was overpowered when his arm was broken by an attacking elephant who destroyed his sword. He fell to the ground and was taken prisoner. Yaugandharayana was placed on a stretcher, his hands were tied, and he was removed from the battle.

As his stretcher was being carried through the city, two palace attendants were trying to clear a path, complaining about the dust and the tumult and the fact that no one was listening to them. 'So much excitement about the princess being abducted that no one wants to hear that noble Yaugandharayana has fallen and been taken prisoner!' 'Here I am,' Yaugandharayana spoke from his stretcher. 'I rescued King Udayana and got rid of all the obstacles in his path. I have had no time for hostility and fear. My plans and strategies have brought honour to my king and disgrace to his enemies. So, I have won, I am victorious! Let everyone see me! I have been brought to this end by my devotion to the king. Let any man who thinks about becoming a minister consider this well!'

A soldier came running to tell Yaugandharayana that Udayana had been captured. 'How can that be?' said Yaugandharayana. 'He left the city on Bhadravati. How was he captured?' 'He was pursued and overtaken by Nalagiri, sir,' replied the soldier. 'Everything depends on the skill of the rider,' said Yaugandharayana. 'We'll see who controls the elephant now.'

'We have orders to take you to the arsenal and keep you there,' said the guards. 'When you had my master here,' taunted Yaugandharayana, 'your guards slept! And now that the treasure has been stolen, you are all alert.' 'Remove his shackles and let him be taken to Minister Bharatarohaka,' shouted the soldier. 'Ah, he hates me,' thought Yaugandharayana. 'His fall began with my success. He could not counter my strategies, he was defeated by my intelligence.'

Bharatarohaka, King Mahasena's chief minister, came to where Yaugandharayana was being held, thinking to himself, 'He did his duty by being deceitful, but I can't bear to see him in this state. How can I gloat when he has come to this by being devoted to his master? His plans were always well conceived, but they did not come to fruition. He's like an angry snake that can only raise its hood and hiss.' Bharatarohaka stepped forward and said, 'I have heard your name, but it is a pleasure to meet you face to face.' 'Yes, look at me now,' said Yaugandharayana, seething, covered with blood but as calm as Dhrishtadyumna after he had killed his father's murderer!'

'Since you succeeded with the help of an elephant, should you be so proud?' asked Bharatarohaka. 'And you?' spat Yaugandharayana. 'What about that false elephant, covered with jasmine and sala branches? And my king bound hand and foot? Is it trickery if my master can charm an elephant with his sitar? How can you blame me if I mimic your tricks?'

'Your master accepted the princess as a student and then ran off with her without even marrying her,' said Bharatarohaka. 'How is that honourable?'

'That's not possible,' said Yaugandharayana. 'King Udayana would never have taken her as a student without marrying her.'

'King Mahasena had showered kindness on King Udayana,' argued Bharatarohaka. 'Why was he not grateful for that?'

'Oh, stop it,' Yaugandharayana was losing patience. 'Nalagiri obeys my king because he is skilled. Your master set him free because he wanted to save his reputation and protect his friends.'

'If your master was set free only to capture the elephant, why was he not imprisoned again?'

'Because your master was afraid of being accused of ingratitude.'

'And what is the punishment for an enemy defeated in battle?'

'It is death,' said Yaugandharayana.

'Well, then, why did we not have your master put to death?' asked Bharatarohaka patiently.

'Because you wanted my master to treat your master well, too,' snapped Yaugandharayana. 'He could have carried him off in an instant. Despite all that you did, King Udayana has escaped – and with your princess.'

The old chamberlain entered and delivered a message from King Mahasena. 'Though you worked many deceits, you played within the rules. I am impressed with your intelligence. I bear you no malice. Accept this gift.' Yaugandharayana bowed his head, thinking, 'I, who should be punished, am honoured.' A commotion was heard outside the arsenal. 'Go and find out what this is all about,' ordered Bharatarohaka. The chamberlain returned with the news that the queen had wanted to kill herself by jumping off the palace balcony. But the king had restrained her, reminding her that by being kidnapped by her lover, her daughter had been married in accordance with acceptable kshatriya rites. He suggested that they celebrate the union in the absence of the bride and groom with a marriage of dolls. The palace women were now running around, gathering auspicious items and objects as they prepared for the marriage rites. 'So King Mahasena has accepted the marriage,' said Yaugandharayana. 'Now you can give me the gift!' 'Is there anything else that the king can do for you?' asked Bharatarohaka with respect. 'I cannot ask for anything more if your king is pleased with me,' said Yaugandharayana, smiling.

THE HOLY MAN AND THE COURTESAN

BY BODHAYANA/MAHENDRAVARMAN

An out-and-out farce, *Bhagavadajjukam* is one of two celebrated and surviving *prahasana*s in classical Sanskrit drama. This comedy conforms perfectly to the conventions of a *prahasana* with one act, a single location and a mere handful of characters who are all rather louche. The central character is an acolyte who wants to know the meaning of life and has chosen a wandering ascetic as his spiritual teacher. Sadly, the teacher and student cannot agree on the how to treat the body even as they cultivate and refine the mind. The playwright appears to be on the side of the acolyte and so, the pompous teacher is gently mocked, as are Yama and his messenger.

The play seems to be from the seventh century CE, and is attributed to Bodhayana. But royal inscriptions tell us that the play was written by the Pallava monarch Mahendravarman (600–630 CE), who ruled in southern India. Mahendravarman was a man of many talents and his reign was a period of high culture. Since he is most certainly the author of the other surviving Sanskrit farce, *Mattavilasa,* it is possible that he wrote *Bhagavadajjukam,* too. Moreover, Mahendravarman was a practising Jain who later became a Shaivite: the satirical presentations of the teacher who endlessly spouts increasingly incomprehensible ideas from Hindu philosophy, as well as the clumsy mistakes of the God of Death and his messenger, are not a surprise if the playwright was not an orthodox Hindu.

List of Important Characters

Bee and Birdie – courtesan's attendants

Courtesan

Mendicant – Shandilya's teacher

Shandilya – mendicant's student

Yama's messenger

The doctor, the courtesan's mother, the courtesan's lover

A mendicant had taken a disciple who was proving to be quite difficult. One morning, the mendicant found the student missing. Thinking he might have gone to get something to eat, he set off to look for him. As he walked along, he called out to his student, 'Shandilya! Shandilya!' even as he cursed the human body and all its frailties, its fevers and its weaknesses, its hungers and thirsts and other physical cravings.

As it turned out, Shandilya was not in the best of moods because he was hungry. He grumbled to himself, 'I was born well, I'm a brahmin. But what good was this sacred thread? We had nothing to eat! I became a Buddhist so that I could eat. But these fellows, they eat only once a day. I was still starving. So I threw away the robe and smashed the begging bowl and now I march around in this loincloth, holding an umbrella. And I've become a slave to this ridiculous teacher. Where is he? I'll bet he went off without me to find something to eat – so he's probably not far away.' Shandilya called out, 'Where are you, good sir? Where are you?'

Teacher and student literally ran into each other, and Shandilya said, 'How do you get your food, master? You know that I took on this life of a mendicant because I wanted to be fed, I have no interest in enlightenment or liberation.' 'What are you saying?' the mendicant was horrified. 'It's the truth,' retorted Shandilya.

'You were the one who told me that lies were fetters, chains . . . ' 'Of course, of course,' said the mendicant quickly. 'The gods guard the good deeds of good men most carefully until they reach a state of detachment, a state in which they have no desires, they don't want things . . . ' 'But how does one not want things?' Shandilya was genuinely perplexed. 'Tch,' the mendicant clicked his tongue in irritation. 'Equanimity – being the same in love and hate, joy and sorrow.' 'But what is this state?' Shandilya persisted. 'Can it actually be reached?' 'Uff,' said the mendicant. 'You refuse to learn!' 'But you don't care, you are free, either way!' shouted Shandilya. 'You know,' said the mendicant, 'they say that a good beating is an effective way to teach a student. I could try that,' and he turned away.

And so, they argued back and forth about the meaning and possibility of detachment and then fell to bickering about whether it was too late to go on their begging rounds. The mendicant said they should go into a nearby garden and rest for a bit. Shandilya pounced on that remark, saying, 'Why? Shouldn't you feel the same, whether you are hungry or sated, tired or energetic?' The poor mendicant then had to launch into a disquisition about the inner soul and the active self: the former was imperishable and unchanging, but the latter experienced the moment with the body, demanding happiness or rest or food. 'Hah!' Shandilya was triumphant. 'See! A man is his body and nothing more!'

Fortunately, by then, they had reached the garden. 'You go first,' said Shandilya. 'My mother told me that a tiger lives in that garden, hidden in the ashoka tree.' The mendicant led the way into the garden, but barely had they entered when Shandilya began to yell, 'Oh! Oh! I've been bitten by the tiger! I will die before I am enlightened! Save me! Save me!' 'That is a peacock, Shandilya!' said the mendicant calmly. 'Why, yes it is!' said Shandilya, and opened his eyes. 'Obviously, that damn tiger was afraid of me and changed himself into a peacock.' 'Oh my!' said the mendicant. 'How lovely this is – look at all the trees and the flowers and the ripe fruits. And oh, the birds and the bees and the sweet breeze!'

'Idiot!' Shandilya muttered. 'The seasons come and go, people regret the past and fear the future. Why do you not learn something more,' the mendicant continued. 'What's the point of learning more?' Shandilya argued.

'From knowledge comes wisdom, from wisdom come self-control and discipline, from self-control comes ascetic practice, which leads to yoga, which gives insight into the past, the present and the future. And that leads to mastery over the Self,' explained the mendicant patiently. 'You think about yoga, sir, I'll think about breakfast,' Shandilya was unredeemed. 'Praise be to the Buddha! In the end, it is to him that I go for refuge!'

As it happened, a courtesan and her attendants, Bee and Birdie, had also come to wander through the garden and enjoy its beauty. Bee was sent off to the city to summon the courtesan's lover while the lady and Birdie sat on a bench and began to sing sweet songs of love. Shandilya heard them and drew closer. 'What a lovely woman!' he thought to himself. 'Ah, she's a courtesan. Damn, the rich are lucky! Master, listen, listen!' 'I shall not listen,' said the mendicant. 'The ear is for hearing, one must recognize the difference between hearing and listening. Now, off with you, I am entering my period of silence for the day.'

It also happened that one of Yama's messengers was approaching the garden. 'I work for the God of Death,' he said to himself proudly. 'I am here to give humans the gift they so richly deserve – the end of life. I have travelled far and wide to get here, to this city, in search of this woman. There she is – made all the more beautiful by the flowers that surround her. She has a few more moments to live, so I'll wait here.'

Birdie remarked on the beauty of the ashoka flowers. 'Let me pluck one for you,' she said. 'No, I'll get it myself,' said the courtesan and reached for the blossoms. 'This is the moment,' said the messenger. 'I will turn myself into a snake and bite her, this creature more lovely than even the dancers in heaven!' 'Ouch!' cried the courtesan. 'Something bit me!' 'There's a snake on that branch!' screamed Birdie. The courtesan fell to the ground. Barely able to breathe, she whispered, 'Remember me to my mother . . . and tell my sweet lover that I embrace him as I die!' 'Master, master,' cried Shandilya. 'She is dead, this lovely woman. I shall mourn her, I shall weep by her body!' He crawled over to where the courtesan lay. 'Oh, let me touch her feet,' wailed Shandilya. 'Her breasts, so firm and up-tilted, were always out of my reach!' Birdie was terribly moved by the sight of this compassionate acolyte, a complete stranger, crying for her mistress. 'I'd better go fetch her mother,' she thought and ran off.

'Stop crying, Shandilya,' said the mendicant. 'This does not become you as a student on the path to liberation!' 'Get away from me, you man who feels no love!' Shandilya continued to wail and caress the courtesan's feet. 'How can she be cured, this poor woman?' 'There is a saying among the Shaivites that compassion generates attachments,' the mendicant said to himself. 'This poor fellow has fallen into that trap. Let me help him see the truth of this matter and gain valuable insight. I'll use all my yogic powers and enter the body of this woman.' The mendicant transported himself into the courtesan's body, leaving his own body lifeless, looking like a corpse.

The courtesan's body spoke. 'Shandilya! Shandilya!' 'You're alive!' shouted Shandilya. 'I am here, madam, I am here!' 'Don't you dare touch me with your unclean hands!' she said. 'But I am so clean,' said Shandilya, surprised. 'Come, sit here and learn a little while you can,' said the courtesan's body. 'Here, too, I have to learn something?' Shandilya thought and then, he noticed the mendicant's corpse. 'Hah! You're dead, too, are you, you blabbering yoga master, you! Well, too bad!'

Birdie arrived in the garden with the courtesan's mother. 'Come, come,' said Birdie. 'She's lying on the ground here, she's been bitten by a cobra. But she's all right.' The mother began to wail. 'How can she be all right? Dear child, dear daughter, what is all this!' The courtesan's body spoke, 'Don't you come near me, you filthy old bawd!' The mother stepped back in surprise. 'The poison must have gone to her brain!' cried Birdie. 'Quick, fetch a doctor!' cried the mother. Bee had just reached the garden with the courtesan's lover. She was saying, 'How she misses you when you are not with her!' 'I miss her too,' sighed the lover. 'My lotus-eyed beauty, I long to drink the nectar of her lips! Ah, here she is. Why is she turning away from me? Darling, darling, look at me!' He pulled at her clothes. 'Hey, let go of my skirt!' said the courtesan. 'What!' cried the lover. 'She has been delirious ever since the snake bit her!' said Birdie. 'My poor dear,' sighed the lover. 'It's as if some puritanical person has entered her body!' The doctor arrived and quickly assessed the situation. 'She's been bitten by a snake and has lost her mind. Never fear, I've dealt with many poisons before.'

He drew a circle and sat in the middle, muttering incantations and charms and talking to things unseen. 'I see,' he said. 'I have to bleed her. Where is my little knife?' 'Hurry up!' snarled the courtesan. 'Some bile as well, eh? Well, water, fire, air – I know how to deal with them all. I'm going to fetch the snake charmer, who has a wide range of pills and potions for all kinds of poisons.'

Yama's messenger came back, muttering to himself, 'That was quite the scolding I got from Yama. "This is not the courtesan whose time was up. Go fetch the right one!" he yelled. But that's not too much of a problem. As long as she hasn't been cremated, I can bring her back to life.' He looked around the area where he had bitten the courtesan and taken her life. 'Well, look at that! Would you believe she's up and about and hale and hearty, even though I still have her life in my hands! Is this a miracle? Not quite – I can see a mendicant who probably has yogic powers, he must be behind all this.' He rubbed his hands with glee. 'Nothing to do but teach him a lesson. I'll just send this woman's life into his body and then we can watch the fun!'

'O Birdie,' cooed the mendicant. Shandilya groaned, thinking, 'He's alive, after all. It's a fact, the truly wretched never die!' 'Where are you, lover boy?' the mendicant trilled. 'I'm feeling a little silly, I think I must be drunk!' 'You're not drunk, you're just plain crazy!' muttered Shandilya. 'Honourable sir, it does not behoove you to speak in this fashion!' said the bewildered lover. 'Another drink?' said the mendicant, who could not be stopped. 'More poison would be good!' said Shandilya, who was beginning to guess what had happened. 'Come here, Birdie, and give me a hug,' sang the mendicant. 'Ugh! You dirty old man!' said Birdie as she moved away. The courtesan's mother appeared, full of concern.

'Why hello there, mother!' lisped the mendicant. 'Good sir, what is this?' cried the mother. 'Are you rejecting me, mother?' replied the mendicant. 'And you, lover boy, you're very slow today!' 'Sir, I'm impotent,' stammered the lover, in desperation.

The doctor came back, huffing and puffing. 'I've brought pills and herbs – this could be instant revival or instant death, there's only one way to find out. Bring us some water while I grind these together. She hasn't been bitten, you know, she's been possessed.' 'You idiot, you don't even know who's dead,' said the courtesan to the doctor. 'What do your books say about snake bites? What are the symptoms?' The doctor fumbled among his things and replied casually, 'There are hundreds of symptoms!' 'No!' snapped the courtesan. 'There are only seven symptoms! And I can also tell you that anyone who displays them is well past the skills and talents of even the celestial physicians. Now, do you have anything useful to say?' 'It certainly looks like you don't need me,' said the doctor, and hurried away.

'Enough of all these games,' said Yama's messenger to himself. 'I should do as my master ordered.' He went up to the courtesan. 'Give it up!' he said firmly. 'With pleasure,' said the mendicant. 'Now I can exchange these poor mixed-up souls,' said the messenger. 'My work here is done!' 'Shandilya! Shandilya!' called the mendicant. 'Wow!' thought Shandilya. 'He's been resurrected. Again!' 'Birdie, sweet Bee!' called the courtesan. 'She is herself again!' chorused Bee and Birdie. 'My daughter!' cried the mother. 'My beloved!' cried the lover, and they all set off happily for the city.

Shandilya turned to the mendicant. 'What was that all about?' 'It's a long story,' his master replied. 'The day is done. I'll tell you when we get home.'

SHAKUNTALA

BY KALIDASA

Kalidasa is believed to have created his great works in the so-called 'golden age' of the Gupta empire in northern India, probably during the reign of Chandragupta Vikramaditya (375–415 CE). Although Kalidasa is a historical figure, there are many legends about his life and many parts of the country, including Kashmir, claim him as their own. Most of these legends begin with the fact that Kalidasa was, in fact, an illiterate and foolish country bumpkin who was seen hacking away at a tree branch upon which he was sitting, oblivious to the fact that when it fell, he would fall with it. It was a subsequent boon from the goddess that bestowed eloquence upon him and thereafter, he took the name Kalidasa, 'slave of the goddess'.

Kalidasa's version of the Shakuntala story from the Mahabharata stands as the paradigmatic *nataka* in Sanskrit literature. The epic story tells of a king who seduced a forest girl with the promise that her son would be the king after him but promptly forgot about her when he returned to the city. When she arrives with her son to claim his birthright, the king insults her and sends her away. But according to the strict rules of writing a *nataka,* Kalidasa needed noble characters for his hero and heroine and a happy ending for the play. In a stroke of writerly genius, Kalidasa inserted a curse, a device that would relieve the king of all blame for his actions and would also complicate the plot of the story just enough to give Kalidasa a perfectly structured seven-act play. Woven into the complications of the curse is the ring of recognition, for which the play is named *Abhijnanasakuntalam,* 'that by which Shakuntala will be recognized'.

List of Important Characters

Aditi – Sage Maricha's wife
Anasuya – Shakuntala's friend
Dushyanta – king of Hastinapura
Durvasas – sage who curses Shakuntala
Gautami – older ascetic woman in Kanva's hermitage
Indra – king of the gods
Kanva – sage who adopted Shakuntala
Madhavya – Dushyanta's companion
Maricha – divine sage
Matali – Indra's charioteer
Menaka – celestial dancer, Shakuntala's mother
Priyamvada – Shakuntala's friend
Sanumati – dancer from Indra's court, Menaka's friend
Sarvadamana – Shakuntala's son
Shakuntala – abandoned baby adopted by sage Kanva
Sharngarva and Sharadvat – young male ascetics from Kanva's hermitage
Vishwamitra – sage known for his fierce ascetic practice, Shakuntala's father

Vishwamitra was immersed in fierce austerities that would help him join the highest rank of sages. The concentration and the determination with which he followed his ascetic practices made Indra, the king of the gods, nervous. So, Indra sent the beautiful apsara, Menaka, most accomplished of all the dancers in heaven, to distract the sage from his purpose. Menaka made herself as seductive as possible and appeared before the sage, dancing and singing softly. Vishwamitra opened his eyes and was unable to resist her charms. The sage and the dancer from Indra's heaven lived together happily in the forest groves and before long, a little daughter was born to them.

Vishwamitra realized that Indra had tricked him into forgetting his great ambition. Enraged, he deserted Menaka and the baby and returned to his solitary life of meditation and austerities. Menaka knew that she could not live in the world of humans forever and so she left her child on the edge of a hermitage, trusting that the good sage who lived there would take care of the baby. The sage, Kanva, found the beautiful baby surrounded by shakunta birds. He took her as his own and named her Shakuntala. The child considered Kanva her father and was devoted to him. She grew up in the hermitage as a simple forest girl along with her two friends, Anasuya and Priyamvada, surrounded by flowering plants and gentle forest creatures.

It happened that one day, King Dushyanta, from the faraway city of Hastinapura, was hunting in the forest that encircled Kanva's hermitage. He began to track a majestic black antelope and as they chased the terrified animal who fled deeper and deeper into the forest, the king and his charioteer were separated from the royal hunting party. Dushyanta's charioteer drew close to the antelope, urging the king to take aim and shoot. Dushyanta drew his bow and was about to release an arrow, sharp and straight, when suddenly, a voice called out. 'Stop, mighty king! This antelope belongs to our hermitage. You cannot kill him!' Two young ascetics appeared from among the trees, saying, 'The weapons you carry, king, should be used to protect the vulnerable and not harm the innocent! Put away your bow and arrows!' Embarrassed, Dushyanta lowered his bow.

One of the young men blessed him. 'May you have a mighty son who will help you rule your great empire!' Dushyanta asked who they were and what they were doing in the forest. They replied that they were disciples of the sage Kanva and were going to collect firewood for his hermitage, which was not far away. They invited the king to visit them and enjoy their hospitality. 'Come and see how your protection nurtures our way of life!' they said. 'Our master is away, but his daughter, Shakuntala, has been put in charge of looking after any guests that may visit us.' The king thanked them and asked his charioteer to proceed in the direction of Kanva's hermitage.

As they drew closer to the sage's small community, the king noticed that the dense forest had given way to gentler vegetation. Wild rice and other edible plants covered the ground, parrots nested in the branches of fruit trees, deer and fawns grazed nearby watching the king and his horses with curiosity rather than fear. A stream burbled somewhere near and Dushyanta thought he could see the gleam of a lily pond in the distance. The king halted the chariot and quickly dismounted. He took off his hunting clothes, his ornaments and his weapons and handing them to his charioteer, said, 'This place is so peaceful, I don't want to carry the scent of the hunt with me. Look after the horses, I'll be back soon.'

As he entered the tranquil space, he felt his arm twitching and wondered to himself, 'Why do I feel this omen of love?' But he was soon distracted by the sweet voices and he hid himself in the bushes. He saw three young women coming toward him, dressed in simple garments, flowers in their hair, clay water pots nestled against their hips. Dushyanta could not help but think how these girls, with their forest clothes and ornaments, far outshone the bejewelled, silk-clad beauties at his court. The girls talked and laughed and teased each other as they watered the young plants at the edge of the grove. Dushyanta learnt that the most lovely among them was Shakuntala, Kanva's daughter. 'This is no sage's daughter,' thought the king. 'She has the bearing of a princess, fit to be my wife! I feel sure of this in my heart, but let me find out more about her.'

As Shakuntala watered a jasmine creeper that had wrapped itself around a sturdy mango tree, a bee, disturbed by her actions, flew out of the leafy vine. Shakuntala was frightened by the bee as it flew around her head and seemed to pursue her. She waved her arms as she cried, 'Oh, save me, save me!' Her friends laughed and said, 'Why don't we call King Dushyanta to save you! After all, this forest and this grove are all protected by him!' Dushyanta seized his chance and emerged from the bushes where he had been hiding. 'How can it be that a young forest maiden is being tormented in my presence!' The girls immediately stopped their light-hearted conversation and ran to make arrangements to honour the unexpected visitor, unsure, despite his royal demeanour, if he was indeed the king.

Shakuntala found her heart fluttering in the presence of this man and so she stood at a distance, hoping that her agitation would not be noticed. Anasuya made bold to ask, 'Who are you, good sir? To which royal clan do you belong? And what brings a man such as yourself, clearly used to finer pleasures, to our forest home?' Dushyanta decided not to reveal the truth about himself and so he replied, 'I have been appointed by our great king to oversee religious matters. I have come here to make sure that your rituals continue without hindrance or disturbance.' The two girls giggled as they looked over at Shakuntala and whispered, 'If only your father were here! He would surely have honoured this important visitor with what is most precious to him!' Dushyanta was puzzled and said, 'The great sage is celibate, he never had a wife. How can this girl be his daughter?'

Anasuya told him the story of Shakuntala's birth and of her real parents, but Shakuntala had become uncomfortable with her friends' banter with the stranger and she turned to leave. Priyamvada, who had sensed the visitor's interest in her friend, said, 'You were going to water these trees for me. Come, pay your debt!' Dushyanta pulled a ring from his finger and said, 'Here, let me pay her debt! But please, don't mistake me for the king. This simply identifies me as a royal official!' Just then, a voice came out of the forest announcing that the king's hunting party had frightened an elephant which had run amok and charged into the hermitage. All residents were asked to stay indoors. The girls went quickly back to their huts.

Dushyanta returned to the hunting party, leaving his heart at the hermitage. Unable to keep his secret to himself, he confessed his love for the forest girl to his companion Madhavya. Madhavya was a man of leisure and pleasure. He was tired of the discomforts of the hunt and missed the luxuries of the palace and the excitement of the city. He was not very sympathetic to his lovelorn friend and mocked him quite mercilessly.

Dushyanta was desperate to visit the hermitage again so that he could be close to Shakuntala and as luck would have it, two young ascetics arrived and asked for an audience with the king. They told the king that Kanva's hermitage was being threatened by *rakshasa*s and needed his protection. The king was overjoyed and prepared to go to the hermitage at once, taking the reluctant Madhavya with him. Just then, a messenger arrived from the city, from the queen herself. She wanted her son, Dushyanta, to be present four days hence when she would celebrate the end of a long period of fasting.

Dushyanta hastened to the hermitage and learnt that his presence had, indeed, kept the rakshasas away and that all the rituals had been completed without disturbance. He also overheard that Shakuntala had been overcome by the heat and was indisposed. Anxiously, he looked around for the girl who haunted his dreams and was somewhat reassured when he spied her in the distance. She was lying on the grass by the river bank while her friends anointed her body with cooling herbal pastes and fanned her with large leaves woven together.

Dushyanta hid himself and watched and listened as Priyamvada and Anasuya whispered among themselves about Shakuntala's condition. Anasuya said to Shakuntala, 'Sweet friend, what is it that ails you? Your behaviour reminds us of the lovers that we have read about in stories! Tell us what's wrong – how can we help you feel better if we don't know what it is that is making you so pale and listless?' Shakuntala replied shyly, 'I'm embarrassed to say this, but I have not been myself since I saw that man, the protector of the hermitage. I am in love, I cannot live without him! Help me to win him over, I beg you!' Dushyanta could barely contain his excitement and it took all his self-control to not jump out and take Shakuntala in his arms.

Priyamvada smiled and whispered to Anasuya that she thought the visitor, too, had romantic intentions towards their friend. Aloud, she said, 'Why not write a love letter that I can hide in a flower? I can pass it to him when we perform our evening worship . . . ' 'Are you sure he feels the same about me?' stammered Shakuntala. 'I couldn't bear it if he did not love me!' 'I'm sure he does,' said Priyamvada. 'He looks rather lovelorn himself! Here, why don't you scratch a love letter onto this leaf with your nail.' Shakuntala hesitated but then said, 'I have composed a short verse: "O, cruel man! I don't know what's in your heart, but I am tortured day and night by my love for you!"'

Delighted with this confession of love, Dushyanta came out from behind the bushes. 'You are tortured by love, dear lady, but I am consumed by it!' he cried. 'Aha!' said Priyamvada. 'Look who's here! It's the king's duty to ease the suffering of his subjects. Let us leave him to make Shakuntala feel better! Come, Anasuya, let's take this fawn to its mother.' Dushyanta embraced Shakuntala and tried to kiss her. But she was shy and pushed him away. 'We can't do this,' she said. 'I cannot give myself to you in this manner!'

'Marry me!' said the king. 'Marry me this minute! We can tell your father later and he will not be angry! Come, let us exchange flower garlands as a sign of our commitment!' A voice came from the direction of the hermitage. Gautami, one of the older women who lived there, called out to Shakuntala, 'It's getting dark, child, come back to the hut!' Hastily, Shakuntala gathered herself and ran toward Gautami, leaving Dushyanta to fall upon the flowers where she had so recently lain.

A few days later, Anasuya and Priyamvada were gathering flowers for the rituals and daily worship, chatting about the new love in their friend's life. 'It's unfortunate that the king had to leave for the city so soon,' said Anasuya. 'I hope he won't forget us when he's back with all his fine women.' 'He's not like that,' said Priyamvada. 'But what do you think father Kanva will say when he hears what has happened in his absence?' 'Well, he had always planned to give his daughter to a worthy husband,' replied Anasuya. 'I think he'll be happy it all worked out like this.' In the distance, they heard someone announce himself. 'I am here!' shouted the voice. 'Oh dear!' said Priyamvada. 'We have a visitor. Shakuntala is here, but her mind and heart are far, far away.'

Before the girls could do anything, they heard the same voice, raised in anger. 'You dare to ignore me! I am a mighty sage! How dare you not greet me! That man you are thinking of, he will forget you, even after he has been reminded!' 'It's Durvasas, the angriest of all sages!' cried Priyamvada. 'Look, he's leaving in a real rage!' She ran after him saying, 'I'll try and pacify him!' She soon returned, looking quite pleased. 'He wouldn't take back the curse, but he did soften it a little. He said the curse would end when the king sees a ring, a token of recognition.' 'That's a relief,' said Anasuya. 'Shakuntala has that ring he gave her on the first day, it has his name on it.'

Days and months went by. Kanva had returned from his travels, but all was not well in the hermitage. Shakuntala sat alone, a picture of sadness, pining for her beloved, from whom she had had no news, not even a single message. But as Kanva approached her, a voice rang out of the sky: 'Know that your daughter holds within her the future of Dushyanta's lineage for the good of the Earth! She is pregnant!' Kanva embraced his sorrowing child and raised her to her feet. 'Weep not, my little one,' he said, gently. 'This very day, I shall send you to your husband with an escort of sages!'

Priyamvada and Anasuya ran around putting things together for Shakuntala's journey, even as tears streamed down their faces. Although this was a moment of great happiness, they were heartbroken at the prospect of being separated from their dear friend. Dressed in her simple forest clothes, her long hair newly washed, Shakuntala stood with her head bowed as the women of the hermitage showered her with grains of rice and their blessings. 'She is going to the city,' sighed Priyamvada. 'Her beauty deserves far more than these forest clothes and ornaments!' Two young boys emerged from the woodland, their arms piled with silks and jewels and lotions and unguents. 'Look what the trees in the hermitage have sent as gifts for Shakuntala in exchange for all the love and care she gave them all these years!'

Priyamvada and Anasuya quickly adorned their beloved friend in the fine silk cloth and the ornaments, painted the soles of her feet with red resin and scented her hair with fragrant oils. They clasped the jewels around her neck, her wrists and her waist and soon, she was fit to meet any royal personage.

Shakuntala bade a tearful farewell to her companions in the hermitage. Then she walked around, seeking the blessings of the trees, the plants and the gentle gods of the forest. She wept as she caressed the little fawn she had rescued and whose injured mouth she had healed, she stroked the flowering vine she had tended with special care. Kanva and all his people walked with her as she set out for the city with the sages, but when they reached the edge of the lake, they knew they could go no further.

Kanva spoke to Sharngarva, the foremost among the ascetics escorting Shakuntala to the city. He said, 'Tell the king, "My daughter fell in love with you before her family could act in the prescribed manner. You are noble – treat my daughter as you do your other wives, give her equal rank. We ask no more than that. The rest is as her destiny wills."' Then he spoke to Shakuntala. 'Be respectful, obedient, friendly, patient, fair and humble. You will have no trouble adjusting to your new family!' Shakuntala embraced her two friends who whispered, 'If the king is slow to remember you, show him the ring he gave you, his signet ring!' 'You scare me with your doubts about my husband,' sobbed Shakuntala. She turned to Kanva. 'Father, dear father, will I ever see this home again?' Kanva stroked her hair and said, 'My child, when you have been queen and raised your son to be a great warrior, your husband will hand over his kingdom and return with you to these tranquil groves!' With a heavy heart, Shakuntala turned away from the only home she had ever known and set her face towards the city.

King Dushyanta had returned to his life in the palace of Hastinapur and become immediately immersed in his royal duties and pleasures. Each morning, he was awakened by sweet songs and gentle music to ease him into the duties and tasks that lay ahead of him. One day, however, the morning song filled him with an unexpected sadness. 'What is this feeling?' he thought to himself. 'I am not separated from anyone that I love, and yet it is true that even a happy man is filled with an unaccustomed sorrow when he sees beautiful things and hears sweet sounds. Could it be that he recalls loves from a previous life, lying deep within his heart?' But the king shook off these thoughts and prepared to meet his chamberlain, who would apprise him of his appointments and meetings. The chamberlain, who was getting old, limped into the king's chambers, leaning on his staff and panting a little. 'Sire, there is a group of ascetics at the palace gate. There are women with them and they wish to see you, for they have a message from the sage Kanva.' 'Tell our royal teacher to greet them with all due honour. I shall meet them in front of the fire altar in our hall of worship,' said Dushyanta. His good spirits had been revived since he had heard the customary praises from his doorkeepers who greeted him each morning.

The ascetics had been talking among themselves as they waited for their audience with the king. Sharngarva said, 'Friend Sharadvat, I know that the king is a good man and that all the citizens live well and follow the prescribed rules of conduct, but I cannot help feeling uneasy. Perhaps I am too used to the serenity of the forest. The city disturbs me.' Sharadvat replied quietly, 'I feel the same way. As if I were in the midst of some great defilement in this city so devoted to pleasure.' Shakuntala, too, was agitated and said to Gautami, 'My right eye is twitching. That is a bad omen!' 'Hush, child,' said Gautami sweetly. 'May the gods of your husband's home turn all discomforts into blessings!' As the forest dwellers walked into the great sacrificial hall, Dushyanta's eyes fell on Shakuntala. He asked the doorkeeper, 'Who is this veiled woman? Why is she in the company of these ascetics?' 'I'm not sure, Your Majesty, perhaps we should look at her more closely,' replied the man. 'Ah, one shouldn't gaze upon the wife of another,' said Dushyanta quickly.

The royal priest introduced the ascetics who hailed the king. They thanked him for his protection and praised him for his just and righteous rule. The king asked after the welfare of sage Kanva and was told that the sage had sent him a message through his disciple. Sharngarva said, 'This is blessed Kanva's message, Your Majesty, "You met my daughter secretly, and you married her, but since I have affection for you both, I forgave you. You are an honourable man and Shakuntala is a virtuous woman. She is now pregnant, accept her as your wife!"'

Gautami interjected before the king could speak. 'She ignored her elders, you did not ask for her hand. You both acted as you pleased. What more is there to say!' 'What are you suggesting?' asked Dushyanta, bewildered. 'A married woman who stays with her family is always doubted, even if she is chaste,' said Sharngarva loudly. 'A wife should live with her husband, even if he has no love for her.' 'Did I marry you?' Dushyanta wondered aloud as he gazed at the woman standing before him with her head bowed in shame.

Gautami pulled off Shakuntala's veil so that the king could see her face. Shakuntala shrank into herself, her heart breaking as her beloved husband looked at her as if she were a stranger. 'I really cannot remember marrying this lady, however hard I try. How can I accept a pregnant woman as my wife when I am not certain that this is my child?' said the king hesitantly. Sharadvat burst out, 'We have delivered our message. The king has said what he has to say.

Show him some proof!' Shakuntala reached for the ring on her finger – but it was bare. 'The ring is lost!' she cried to Gautami. 'It must have fallen off when you bathed in the sacred waters!' replied Gautami, her voice shaking with distress. 'This woman is a liar and a temptress!' said the king. 'You are a wicked man, hiding behind a show of justice,' retorted a weeping Shakuntala. 'I came here because I had faith in your noble lineage, but in you, I have found only deceit!' 'Take her or leave her,' said Sharngarva to the king. 'She is now in your power, whether you want her or not!' Seeing that the king was not going to accept that he had married a forest girl, Sharngarva and Sharadvat turned to leave. 'How can you abandon me!' sobbed Shakuntala as the ascetics left the great hall of worship.

The king turned to the royal priest and said, 'Help me! I don't know what to do. Am I deluded? Is she telling the truth? I have no way to tell.' The priest replied, 'Let this woman stay in the palace until her child is born. It has been foretold that your eldest son will be born with all the auspicious marks of a great emperor. If her child is born bearing those marks, you will know that he is yours and you can accept the woman as your wife and claim your son. But if the child is born without these marks, send the woman back to her father.' The king was happy to follow this plan, which seemed reasonable and entirely to his advantage. He instructed his courtiers to take Shakuntala into the women's quarters. As she was led away, Shakuntala called piteously on Mother Earth to swallow her.

Order was restored so that the king could resume his duties. Just then, a disembodied voice was heard shouting, 'Amazing! A miracle!' The priest came running back into the hall. 'Sire, Sire!' he panted. 'Something incredible has happened. That woman was wailing and crying and then, a ray of light in the shape of a woman appeared and carried her away into the sky!' The king shook his head in disbelief and decided he had had enough for the day. He called upon his doorkeepers to lead him back to his private chambers. 'I don't remember marrying that girl,' he thought. 'But there is a pain in my heart that makes me feel I might have!'

Sometime later, a thief was dragged into the city magistrate's court by two policemen. 'Where did you get that jewelled ring with the king's name engraved on it, you dog?' shouted one of the policeman as he cuffed the thief across the side of his head. 'Tell us, in front of the honourable magistrate!' 'I'm a fisherman, not a thief!' whimpered the man. 'I was cutting up a fish I had caught, and I found the ring in its belly. I pulled it out and went to sell it. That's where you found me, now I'm here. End of story! Let me go!' 'Guard this fellow closely,' said the magistrate. 'I'll take this ring to the king. Let him decide what needs to be done with this fool!' The magistrate took a long time to return, but when he did, he was holding a bag of money. 'The king has sent you the price of the ring,' he said to the fisherman. 'Take it and be off!' 'The king must really value this ring,' said one of the policemen. 'I don't know about that,' replied the magistrate. 'But he was very disturbed when he saw the ring, he said it made him think of someone he had loved.'

One day, a dancer from Indra's court, Sanumati, came down to earth. 'I have come here to help Shakuntala, Menaka's daughter,' she said to herself as she looked around. 'I wonder where she could be. But why are there no signs of the Spring Festival? Surely King

Dushyanta has not forgotten this auspicious day! Let me see what I can find out.' She saw two young palace maids going into the pleasure gardens and she followed them. The maids plucked the tender leaves of a mango tree waiting to flower and were weaving them together when the old chamberlain appeared. He shook his stick at them as he scolded, 'What are you doing? Don't you know that the king has forbidden the celebration of Spring?' The maids dropped the leaves and buds they had gathered, but they could not contain their curiosity and asked, 'But why?' 'Ever since the king saw the ring he had given Shakuntala, he has not been himself. He mopes and sighs and curses himself for having rejected the woman he loved. He can barely accomplish his royal duties.' 'Oh, I am delighted to hear this,' thought Sanumati.

Just then, the king, wearing only a single bracelet and no ornaments at all, wandered into the garden, his face dulled by sadness. Sanumati was struck by his good looks, even though he was pale and wan. 'I can see why Shakuntala is in love with him. And he too, seems to be pining for his beloved,' she thought. She followed the king as he walked through the gardens with his friend Madhavya and eventually sat down in an arbour filled with flowers. Dushyanta recalled over and over again how he had rejected Shakuntala and how sad and humiliated she had looked. Madhavya could do nothing to raise his spirits, not with his silly jokes nor with assurances that the reappearance of the ring surely meant that the king would be with Shakuntala again soon. Sanumati listened to the king's conversation with Madhavya, pleased that he was filled with remorse and seemed to truly love Shakuntala as he recalled how happy he had been with her for those few short days in the forest. Sanumati had seen enough of the king's grief and so she returned to her own realm to tell her friend, Menaka, that her daughter had not been abandoned by the king in favour of someone else.

Suddenly, Dushyanta heard Madhavya in the distance, screaming that he was being murdered. A doorkeeper rushed in, shouting, 'Madhavya needs your help! He has been carried away by a celestial being!' At once, the king asked for his bow and arrows and rushed off to where the commotion was. He could see nothing but drew his bow, ready to loose an arrow at whoever had abducted his dear friend. Matali, Indra's charioteer, appeared before him and said, 'I picked up Madhavya to make you angry and to shake you out of your despondency. I have a message from Indra. Demons descended from Kalanemi, who are invulnerable to Indra, are attacking. Prepare for battle on behalf of the gods! Mount Indra's chariot and come away with me!' The king left his kingdom in the charge of his ministers and hurried away with Matali. Dushyanta defeated the demons and was richly rewarded by Indra and honoured by all the heavenly beings.

As he flew through the skies with Matali on his way back to Hastinapura, Dushyanta saw a beautiful mountain that shone like gold. The divine sage Maricha lived there with his wife, Aditi. The king told Matali that he wished to pay his respects to the sage. The sage was engaged in his daily rituals and as Dushyanta waited in the hermitage, a boy ran into the clearing, tugging at the mane of a lion cub and playing roughly with the young animal. Dushyanta was overcome with emotion. 'I have no son, why does my heart go out to this beautiful child? He seems quite extraordinary. And look! He carries all the marks of a great emperor on his body! Ah, fathers who have sons are so fortunate!' he sighed. 'Is this child the son of some great sage?' he asked the ascetic women who had followed the boy. 'Oh, my!' said one of the women. 'This boy looks exactly like you. And even though he doesn't know you, he is easy in your company! He is not the son of a sage – he is born in the line of kings.' Dushyanta's heart skipped a beat – could it be that this child . . . ? Suddenly, one of the women cried out, 'Where is that amulet the boy wears all the time?' She grew extremely agitated and started to look for it. Dushyanta saw it lying in the dirt and went to pick it up. 'Don't touch it!' shouted the women together. But it was too late – Dushyanta held the amulet in his hand. 'What is the matter?' he asked. 'No one but this child or his parents can touch this amulet if it falls to the ground,' they replied, their eyes wide with wonder. 'If someone other than these three were to touch it, that person would turn into a snake! But nothing has happened to you!' Dushyanta was completely overcome and embraced the little boy. The boy struggled and cried, 'I want my mother!'

As if she had heard the boy, Shakuntala came into the grove dressed in the garments of an ascetic woman, her long hair in a single braid. 'Who is the strange man who calls me his son and wants to hold me in his arms?' cried the boy, running to his mother. Shakuntala looked long and carefully at the king, who had grown thin and pale in his sorrow. Her eyes filled with tears when she recognized her beloved husband. 'Good husband,' she whispered. Dushyanta fell at her feet and begged her to forgive him. Shakuntala raised him up, asking, 'But how do you recognize me now? What has caused you to remember me as your wife?' She saw the signet ring on his finger. 'Oh, how much I tried to tell you who I was when this ring was lost!' 'I remembered everything when I saw the ring again,' said the king. 'I have thought of you every single minute since then!'

Matali arrived. 'Ah! You are all united. Come! The sage Maricha and his wife wish to see you.' The divine sage and his wife blessed the family, showering good wishes and boons upon them all. Dushyanta apologized for having married Shakuntala without permission and then for having failed to recognize her as his wife when she came to his court, pregnant with their child. Maricha consoled him, saying, 'When Menaka brought this bewildered young woman to us from your palace, I went into a meditative trance and saw that you had forgotten Shakuntala because of Durvasas' curse. I also learned that you would remember everything when you saw your signet ring.' Dushyanta sighed with relief. 'So, I am not to blame,' he said. 'And,' said Shakuntala, 'I am glad to know that my husband did not reject me for no reason, even though I don't remember being cursed. But my friends at the hermitage did tell me to show him the ring . . . ' Her voice trailed off. 'All is well now,' said Maricha. 'The darkness of the curse has been lifted and your family is united. This boy, your son, is destined to be a great emperor. We call him Sarvadamana, but when he rules the earth, he will be known as Bharata, the Sustainer.' The sage's wife, Aditi, said, 'Look, here comes Menaka to celebrate this happy occasion. Send a message to Kanva so that he, too, can join us.' Maricha asked, 'Is there anything else you need to be completely happy?' 'Nothing more,' said Dushyanta. 'Let kings protect the world, let priests honour the gods and let Shiva destroy my cycle of rebirths!'

THE MINISTER'S SIGNET RING

BY VISHAKHADATTA

Chanakya, a skilled and wily brahmin, has become minister to Chandragupta, the young man who founded the Mauryan empire in 326 BCE. Now, Chanakya must ensure that Chandragupta is safe and that the newly won kingdom is secure from both internal and external enemies. But Chanakya has a rival – the honourable minister, Rakshasa, who had served the previous rulers, the Nandas, with skill and alacrity. As Chanakya orchestrates a series of deceits and betrayals, Rakshasa tries to rally the last of the Nanda's allies and the men who had served them loyally from within the kingdom into a counter-insurgency movement that will topple the Maurya. Everyone lives in fear of Chanakya, no one knows whom to trust, spies are everywhere, and a tiny mistake can mean the difference between life and death.

Vishakhadatta probably lived in the sixth century CE, and the names of his father and grandfather indicate that his family was associated with some level of administration. Growing up around something that resembled a court, however small, seems to have given Vishakhadatta the knowledge (if not the actual experience) he needed to give *Mudrarakshasa* its ring of authenticity, if you will excuse the pun. This is certainly the most realistic of all the plays in this volume, and what it may lack in terms of gentle romance is more than made up for by the incredibly complex plot that holds together all the various conspiracies.

List of Important Characters

Bhadrabhatta and Bhagurayana – Chanakya's men
Chanakya – Chandragupta Maurya's prime minister
Chandanadasa – jeweller, friend of Rakshasa
Chandragupta – Mauryan emperor
Jishnudasa – jeweller, friend of Rakshasa
Jivasiddhi – Jain monk, close to Rakshasa
Malayaketu – Parvata's son
Nipunaka – Chanakya's spy
Parvata – Chandragupta's ally
Rakshasa – prime minister to the defeated Nandas
Sharngarva – Chanakya's student
Shakatadasa – Rakshasa's close friend
Siddharthaka – Chanakya's fixer
Viradhaka – snake charmer, Rakshasa's spy

Chanakya, minister and loyal counsellor to the emperor Chandragupta Maurya, was sitting alone outside his house, thinking about the events of the last few months. The Nandas had been ousted and Chandragupta was on the throne, but there was still much to do to make him entirely secure. Rakshasa, who had been the Nandas' prime minister, was a good man and skilled in the art of governance. But as long as he was there, he would be a threat to the new ruler. Many from the old regime had gathered around him, for he was a natural leader and commanded respect as well as loyalty. Rakshasa had made several attempts on Chandragupta's life: once, he sent in a *vishakanya*, a 'poison maiden', to seduce the emperor and kill him with the poisons she carried on her body. Chanakya had diverted her attention to Parvata, who had been Chandragupta's ally when he defeated the Nandas. Chanakya passed the blame for that murder onto Rakshasa, who then had to flee the capital city of Pataliputra.

Malayaketu, Parvata's son, had secretly been told the truth about who had really killed his father, but as he was surrounded by spies, there was little he could do. In another attempt, Rakshasa had hidden assassins in a tunnel that led to Chandragupta's private chambers. But Chanakya had foiled that conspiracy as well. He had noticed a trail of ants coming out of the walls carrying crumbs of fresh food. That led him to where the killers were hiding and he had them burned to death. There had even been an attack on Pataliputra by a group of neighbouring kings, though Chandragupta and his forces had defeated them quite easily. Chanakya was pleased with all that he had done, but there were enough reasons, he thought, to remain on guard against the dangers that still lurked, shadowing the new monarch and his court.

Chanakya's thoughts were interrupted by his student, who had come to announce the arrival of a visitor. Recognizing the visitor as Nipunaka, one of his spies, Chanakya asked him what he had learned about the people's feelings towards Chandragupta. Nipunaka assured him that Chandragupta was gaining popularity and that there were only three people whose hearts were not yet with the king. One was a Jain monk called Jivasiddhi, who had become very close to Rakshasa. Another, Shakatadasa, was also Rakshasa's close friend. Chanakya smiled to himself. Jivasiddhi was already his informant and he knew that he could very quickly neutralize Shakatadasa. 'There is a third man, sir,' said Nipunaka. 'Rakshasa left his wife at Chandanadasa's house when he fled the city.' 'How do you know that?' asked Chanakya. 'This ring should tell you everything,' said Nipunaka. Chanakya examined the ring and could not believe his good fortune. 'Where did you get this?' he asked. 'I disguised myself as a priest and went to his shop and started chanting like any other priest,' said Nipunaka, gleefully. 'A little boy ran out of the back of the shop and came to where I was. This seemed to cause a great disturbance. I could hear women calling and scolding. One of the women ran out, picked up the boy and took him away. But in all that fuss, this ring slipped from her finger and rolled over to where I was. It's a man's ring and when I saw that it had Rakshasa's name on it, I knew I had to bring it to you.' 'Well done, my man!' said Chanakya as he closed his fist over the ring.

Once again, Chanakya gathered his thoughts. 'I think I have what I need to finally defeat Rakshasa. I have just sent the honourable brahmin Vishvavasu and his brother to take a share in Parvata's wealth and jewels that the king is distributing to ensure the dead man's safe passage into the afterlife. That is step one. I have also heard that Rakshasa has gathered the support of five kings against Chandragupta. I wonder if I should name them all in the letter I am about to write, using this one stone to kill five birds. Perhaps not. Let me leave it vague. This is step two. Let me put my plan into action.' He summoned his student, Sharngarva, and said, 'I am working on a matter of great consequence and I need your undivided attention as well as your sworn loyalty. Go to Siddharthaka and tell him that you have come from me. Tell him that learned scholars like myself have the worst handwriting and so he should go to Shakatadasa and ask him to write this letter.' Chanakya whispered the contents of the letter into Sharngarva's ear. 'There should be no address on the outside because someone is going to take this letter to someone else, along with a verbal message. And, most importantly, Siddharthaka should not tell Shakatadasa that it is I, Chanakya, who has asked for this letter to be written. Go, now!'

Soon after, Siddharthaka came to Chanakya with the letter in his hand. Chanakya made Siddharthaka seal it with Rakshasa's signet ring and said, 'Sharngarva, go to the city police chief and tell him that I said that the king has commanded that the Buddhist monk named Jivasiddhi be banished from the kingdom for the crime of murdering Parvata by using the vishakanya procured by Rakshasa. Let this be publicly proclaimed for all to hear and then let the sentence be carried out. And further, tell him that Shakatadasa, who has been conspiring against the king, should be impaled on a stake and that his family should be imprisoned. Let this also be publicly proclaimed and then carried out.' When Chanakya had instructed his student thus, the young man went off to carry out his task.

'What should I do with this letter?' asked Siddharthaka. 'You, my friend, will go to the execution grounds and frighten the executioners with frowns and whispers. And when they leave their posts in confusion, you will abduct Shakatadasa and take him quickly and safely to Rakshasa's house. Rakshasa will think of you as his ally and will reward you. Take the reward and stay at his house as his personal companion and assistant. And then, when the time is right, this is what you have to do.' Chanakya whispered further instructions in Siddharthaka's ear. 'As you say, sir,' said Siddharthaka and hurried away.

Sharngarva returned with the news that the police chief was ready to act on the king's commands. Chanakya then sent him to fetch Chandanadasa, the jeweller who was Rakshasa's close friend. When the jeweller heard that he had been summoned by Chanakya, he thought to himself, 'My goodness, even an innocent man like me quakes with fear when I am called into the presence of Prime Minister Chanakya! What must guilty men feel!' Before he left home, he called for one of his associates, a Buddhist, who lived in the same quarter and said, 'I fear that Chanakya will raid my home and shop. Please take Rakshasa's family away to a safe place.'

Chanakya welcomed Chandanadasa warmly. He gave him a seat of honour and asked after his business. And then he asked him if he was loyal to Chandragupta. 'Of course, my lord,' replied Chandanadasa. 'Who would not be loyal to our noble monarch? He is like the full moon in all its glory, lighting up the world.' 'Well, you are so loyal that you've been hiding Minister Rakshasa's family in your home, I believe,' said Chanakya smiling, but without mirth. 'That does not speak to the king's benefit.' 'People spread rumours, sir,' stammered Chandanadasa. 'When men are ousted from their positions of power,' said Chanakya, 'they often panic and flee, leaving their family with their trusted friends, you know.' 'Yes, yes, that is what happened,' said the jeweller. 'There was a panic, and the family was left at my house . . . ' 'But,' said Chanakya, toying with the jeweller, 'you said they were never there, and now you say they are? Which is it? In any case, where are they now?' 'I can honestly say that I don't have that information,' said Chandanadasa, relieved, and turned towards the noise that came in through the open window.

Sharngarva bustled in and told Chanakya that Jivasiddhi, the monk who had been accused of treason, was being banished from the kingdom immediately. Chanakya sighed. 'Even a monk, eh? Our king has no patience with traitors,' he said looking at Chandanadasa meaningfully. 'Just give up Rakshasa's family and all will be well. You will enjoy the king's favour for as long as you live.' 'Sir,' replied Chandanadasa, 'as I said, the minister's family are no longer with me, and I do not know where they are.'

The commotion on the street grew louder and Sharngarva appeared again with the news that this time, Shakatadasa, traitor to the king, was to be impaled on the stake and that crowds of people were following him to watch the execution. Chanakya tried to cajole the jeweller. 'Mr Jeweller, Mr Rich Man, you can see that the king has no patience with those that plot against him, those that seek his downfall. He will show you no mercy. Now come on, save your own life and that of your wife by telling me where Rakshasa's family is.' 'Even if I knew where they were, I would not tell you,' replied the jeweller calmly. 'I see you have made up your mind,' said Chanakya. 'I admire you. Who, other than King Shibi, would give up all that he would gain in order to protect others? Very well, so it shall be. Sharngarva, tell the governor to seize this man's wealth and property and to throw him and his wife into prison. I will confer with His Majesty, who will, no doubt, have them executed.' Chandanadasa stood up. 'Do all that your power allows you to do, prime minister,' he said. 'I am proud that I am being punished not for my own deeds but for the sake of my friends!' He left the room with his head held high. Chanakya rubbed his hands together with glee. 'Hah!' he muttered. 'I have Rakshasa now. I have him where I want him!'

'Sir, sir,' cried Sharngarva, rushing in again, greatly agitated. 'Just as Shakatadasa was about to be impaled, that Siddharthaka ran away with him!' Chanakya hid his smile and said to his student, 'What! Immediately, tell Bhagurayana to go after him and find him at any cost!' 'Sir, Bhagurayana has also disappeared,' wailed Sharngarva. 'Find Bhadrabhatta! Get him and his men to follow these scoundrels!' Chanakya was pleased that things were unfolding according to his plans. 'But he left before dawn this morning with all his men! Oh, oh, everything is in a mess,' cried Sharngarva, distraught. 'They are gone for their own reasons,' said Chanakya calmly. 'I will see to it that those who have remained work for the benefit of our king.' And to himself, he said, 'Let my talent, my skills and my cunning not forsake me now. They were enough to bring down the Nandas. Let them now work to secure this kingdom. I will find you, Rakshasa – you with your great mind and your resources and your charisma and your finely honed skills – and I will bring you to Chandragupta!'

Minister Rakshasa was also assessing the events of the past few months. He was restless, unable to sleep since the once-powerful Nandas had been defeated and he chafed at having to serve under a stranger. 'I still apply my mind to stratagems and plans, I remain loyal, I stay away from sensual pleasures, I am not afraid for my life nor do I seek personal gain – all so that my former masters, wherever they are in the afterlife, might have the satisfaction of seeing their enemy fall. Ah, Goddess of Fortune, you fickle creature, how could you abandon the great Nandas and turn your attention to that upstart? Have you no recognition of merit? Even with so many well-born and illustrious kings around, you have chosen that low-born Maurya! Well, he is the very one that I'm going to get rid of, this favoured prince of yours! I did the right thing by leaving my family with my dear friend Chandanadasa when I fled the city. Those who are still loyal to the Nandas will know that I care about what happens to Pataliputra. I've given enough money to Shakatadasa to ensure that assassins and poisoners will keep making attempts to murder Chandragupta and still more money to seduce the disgruntled men on the Mauryas' side. Then, there's Jivasiddhi, who's creating a network of spies to keep us informed of every blink, every scratch, in the enemy camp.'

Rakshasa's thoughts were interrupted by Malayaketu's chamberlain, who hobbled in, complaining about old age and his creaking joints. Rakshasa offered him a seat and as he sat down, he said, 'I have come from Prince Malayaketu, who is with you in your distress about the overthrow of the Nandas. But he says that you must no longer forego all jewels and ornaments. He sends you one of his own as a gift.' Rakshasa thanked the old man and said, 'I had sworn I would not adorn my body as long as that uncouth man was on the throne. But he will soon be vanquished, and so, please tell the prince that I accept his gift and that I will not disappoint him.'

There was another visitor immediately after the chamberlain left. A snake charmer arrived at the door and asked to see Rakshasa. Rakshasa was scarcely in the mood to be entertained by snake tricks and so he asked the man to leave. But the snake charmer persisted and said that he was a poet. He handed the attendant a poem to give to the minister. 'A bee uses its skill to draw honey from the flowers, but the honey is used by others with fruitful results.' Rakshasa understood that the snake man was a spy and called him in. He asked his attendants to leave. Then he said, 'Tell me, Viradhaka, what's happening in the city with our assassins and killers? Tell me everything from the moment Chandragupta stepped into the Nanda's palace.'

The snake charmer launched into his account of all that had happened. 'His Majesty, the Nanda Sarvarthasiddhi, could not bear the suffering of his besieged citizens and so, he left the city by an underground tunnel. In the confusion that followed, his ally, King Parvata, was killed by the vishakanya you sent to poison Chandragupta. Parvata's son, Malayaketu, ran away as soon as he heard of his father's death. Chanakya then told the royal carpenter to renovate the eastern gates to celebrate Chandragupta's victory. The new king entered the city at the stroke of the midnight hour, accompanied by Vairodhaka, Parvata's brother, to whom Chanakya had promised half the kingdom. He was wonderfully clothed, covered in flowers and jewels and wearing the most magnificent fabrics from head to toe – even his closest friends would not have recognized him. He was mounted on Chandragupta's own elephant and was placed ahead of all the Maurya allies in the procession.

All kinds of preparations had been made to greet Chandragupta: the carpenter, who is our man, was to drop a mechanical device upon him that would kill him, the mahout was prepared to stab him with his dagger, and so on. But the elephant took an unexpected side step and the device fell on the mahout and killed him. The carpenter jumped down and tried to compensate for the fatal error by stabbing Vairodhaka, but the crowd stoned the carpenter to death.' 'This is terrible,' sighed Rakshasa. 'Such good men, my allies, all dead! But what about the physician, Abhayadatta? Did he manage to kill Chandragupta?' 'He carried out the plan of the poisoned drink and gave it to Chandragupta in a golden bowl. But Chanakya noticed that the drink had changed colour. He declared it a poison and made Abhayadatta drink it. It was awful!' said the snake charmer. 'And then that fool, Pramodaka, he lived a flashy life with all the money you had given him and when he was questioned about the source of his income, he was unable to give a coherent answer. Chanakya had him put to death by torture.' 'What about Bibhatsaka and his band of men, who hid in the tunnel that led to Chandragupta's private chambers?' asked Rakshasa quietly, fearing the worst. 'Oh dear, they suffered the most terrible fate of all,' came the reply. 'Chanakya went to inspect the private chambers before Chandragupta was allowed to sleep there. He noticed a line of ants coming out of a hole in the wall carrying grains of boiled rice – that's how he knew that there were assassins hiding in the room. He started a fire and the men were trapped. Blinded by smoke, they could not find their way out and were burned to death.' 'Truly, good fortune is in love with Chandragupta!' said Rakshasa. 'Sir, noble men do not give up their plans because they are repeatedly stalled by obstacles,' the snake charmer insisted. 'We must persist! Chanakya has become even more suspicious and watches everyone and everything. He has gone after our other friends, too – Jivasiddhi has been banished from the kingdom for sending the vishakanya to Parvata and I hear that Shakatadasa is to be impaled for killing the carpenter.' 'Ah, Chanakya,' said Rakshasa, 'how well you have covered your own tracks!' And he put his head in his hands. 'There is more, sir,' continued the snake charmer. 'Your friend Chandanadasa has been arrested, along with his wife and son and thrown into jail. His business has been confiscated, too. He refused to give up your family to Chanakya – he managed to send them away before he was questioned.'

Rakshasa's attendant entered the room. 'Shakatadasa is here to see you, sir,' he said. 'How can this be?' said Rakshasa, rising from his seat. 'But if it is true, bring him in, bring him in!' Shakatadasa came in, followed by Siddharthaka. Rakshasa embraced his friend, holding him close for a long time. 'You are alive!' said Rakshasa. 'Yes,' said Shakatadasa, 'this man, Siddharthaka, saved me from the executioners.' Rakshasa took one of his ornaments and held it out to Siddharthaka. 'Thank you, sir,' said Siddharthaka. 'But I am new here and I know no one with whom I might leave this for safekeeping. This and this other ornament I have, I would like to leave them in your custody.' He pulled a ring out from his clothes and gave it to Rakshasa, who recognized it as his own, the one his wife had taken with her as comfort in his absence. 'Where did you get this?' he asked. 'I found it on the ground outside the house of some jeweller,' said Siddharthaka. 'My friend, this is Minister Rakshasa's signet ring,' said Shakatadasa. 'You must return it to him, and your reward will be many times the value of the ring itself!' 'You keep it, friend,' said Rakshasa to Shakatadasa. 'Use it for official business.' Siddharthaka had another request. 'Sir, I cannot return to Pataliputra now that I have angered Chanakya. Please, let me enter your service as an attendant.' Rakshasa was happy to have this good and brave man in his employ and had the other attendants lead him away.

Rakshasa turned to the snake charmer. 'Tell me, Viradhaka, do the people of the city see what we are doing? Are they on our side?' 'Yes, they are, some of them,' said Viradhaka. 'They also see that Chandragupta was not pleased when Malayaketu escaped. And it seems as if Chanakya has started to ignore Chandragupta's orders and does more and more as he pleases.' 'Good,' said Rakshasa. 'Now, go back to the city and meet the poet, Stanakalasha. Tell him to compose verses that praise the king and turn him against Chanakya. And to send us messages whenever he can.' Viradhaka went back to his disguise as a snake charmer and returned to the city.

'I can have hope,' thought Rakshasa to himself. 'Chandragupta and Chanakya are sure to clash – one will do anything to remain king and the other is obsessed with wiping out the Nandas.'

In the palace, Chandragupta's chamberlain was trying to get things organized for the Kaumudi full moon festival that the new monarch wanted to celebrate. He was bustling through the rooms and hallways, telling courtiers and retainers about decorations and festivities. Chandragupta entered, complaining mildly about the burdens of kingship which had so many aspects, primarily the welfare of the people and the propitiation of the whimsical Goddess of Sovereignty. 'There is already so much to do. And now, I have received a message from my mentor, Chanakya, that I am to fake a disagreement with him and pretend to govern entirely by my own wishes for a while. Of course, I've agreed to do this even though I'm not sure what his larger plan is.' Chandragupta had been preoccupied with these thoughts, but when he walked through the palace which was bathed in gentle autumn moonlight and overflowing with an abundance of seasonal fruit and flowers and grains and produce, he was soothed by the beauty around him.

Chandragupta went to the palace terrace and looked out over the city. To his surprise, it was quiet. 'Where are all the people?' he asked the chamberlain. 'Why is the Kaumudi festival not being celebrated? I had given specific orders that all the citizens should enjoy these days with performances and fairs and visits to temples and shrines.' The chamberlain said nothing. 'Has someone countermanded my orders?' 'There is only one person who could do that, Your Majesty,' said the chamberlain. 'Would that be Chanakya? Well, bring him to me at once,' said the king.

The chamberlain ambled off to where Chanakya lived. As before, he was struck by the austere dwelling, more like the home of a forest sage than that of a prime minister of a wealthy kingdom. Chanakya was thinking about Rakshasa's latest moves in their power game. 'You do not know who you are up against, Rakshasa! My king is not a decadent Nanda who lets ministers do the governing. And you are no Chanakya,' he thought to himself. 'My men are everywhere, they surround Malayaketu and even Rakshasa himself. I've already pretended to disagree with Chandragupta – that should create a rift between Rakshasa and Malayaketu. I can be patient, for I am in a strong position.'

The chamberlain approached Chanakya with his message from the king. 'The king wants to see me?' replied Chanakya. 'Does he already know that I rescinded his orders about the Kaumudi festival? Was it you who told him that, chamberlain?' The chamberlain began to quake in his shoes, but Chanakya stood up and went with the old man to the palace. The new king and his wily counsellor greeted each other formally and exchanged pleasantries until Chandragupta finally said, 'Why did you cancel the Kaumudi celebrations?' 'Your Majesty,' replied Chanakya, 'There are three kinds of government – by the king alone, by the ministers, and the third, where the king and the ministers govern together, as we do. Why do you question my actions?'

Chanakya was distracted by the two bards who were singing for the king. He was disturbed by the songs – the first one was the usual panegyric that asked the gods to bless the monarch, but the second one reminded the king to crush those that were disloyal to him. Then, it struck him that this was one of Rakshasa's ploys. Chandragupta gave the bards a fair amount of money, saying how pleased he was with their songs. Chanakya made it clear that he disapproved of the great size of the sum. Chandragupta was a little irritated that Chanakya was being critical of his smallest actions and asked again why the Kaumudi festival had been cancelled. 'I forbade it so that your orders would be countermanded – a ruler gains more from humility than he does from pride. And there is another reason, too. Sonottara! Bring the list of palace officials that have pledged allegiance to Malayaketu! Look here,

My Lord – these two, who cared for your elephants and horses, were decadent drunks. These two and this one – they were greedy and wanted more money. This one told Malayaketu that I was responsible for his father's death. And these two, they were simply jealous of your success.' 'If you knew all this, why didn't you arrest them?' asked Chandragupta. 'It's not that simple to arrest people, you must have good reasons,' said Chanakya. 'The two ways to deal with such disaffected people – with favour or with punishments – both were out of the question in these cases. None of these men would have been satisfied with any favour that we showed them and there was no reason to punish them. If we had punished our own officials, our people would have lost faith in us. Besides, with Rakshasa's advice, Malayaketu is preparing to attack us with the armies of five kings and all these men are with him. This is not the time for feasting and celebrating. We need to concentrate on our defences.'

Chandragupta was still being petulant. 'Why did you let Rakshasa escape when we had him right here in the city?' he demanded. 'Rakshasa is well-respected and still has the admiration of many people who used to support the Nandas. And he has a great many resources in terms of both men and money. I thought he would only make trouble if he stayed in the city, so I let him escape. It would be easier to manage him if he were outside . . . ' Chandragupta interrupted: 'You could have neutralized him while he was here, you could have taken him by force – so many options were available to you!' 'I did not want him to come to any harm,' Chanakya said, controlling his mounting anger. 'We have to subdue him as one would subdue a wild elephant in the jungle.' 'Who can contradict you, honourable teacher?'

said Chandragupta, with a trace of sarcasm. 'But I do think that Rakshasa has got the better of us, and he has me so confused with his grand strategies that I don't know who to trust.' 'Better of us? Who do you think ousted the Nandas?' Chanakya was almost shouting. 'You think you got rid of the Nandas?' taunted Chandragupta. 'Who was the one who took a public vow to annihilate the enemy and his clan?' said Chanakya indignantly. 'Who undid his topknot and swore vengeance? Who slaughtered the nine Nandas with all their wealth in front of Rakshasa?' 'It was their fate!' Chandragupta said, refusing to back down. 'Only fools believe in fate!' Chanakya cried. 'Yes, and the wise are not boastful!' retorted Chandragupta. 'You are scolding me as if I were a lowly retainer! How dare you!' Chanakya's face was red with rage and his breath came fast and heavy. 'Dear teacher,' Chandragupta said. 'You are really angry.' Chanakya calmed himself. 'If you think Rakshasa is so great, greater than me, here, give him this sword and let him be your counsellor.' He threw his sword on the ground and left the room. 'Rakshasa!' he said to himself. 'You think you have sown the seeds of disunion between me and the king. But this will come back to haunt you!'

Chandragupta called his chamberlain. 'Proclaim that from now, Chandragupta will rule the kingdom without Chanakya!' The chamberlain trembled. 'What are you waiting for!' shouted Chandragupta. The chamberlain hurried off. Chandragupta asked to be escorted to his private chamber. 'I have such a headache from this charade of an argument,' he thought. 'I feel so terrible for having spoken like this to my teacher, even though it was all a pretence.' The king walked to his sleeping quarters, his head low and his eyes on the ground.

Rakshasa was spending sleepless nights, fretting about Chanakya's schemes and stratagems. He was tired and worn from worrying but he had to remain vigilant. One day, his doorkeeper announced a visitor, Karabhaka from Pataliputra. But even as Rakshasa was trying to remember what task he had assigned to Karabhaka, Prince Malayaketu was announced from the other door. He had left his retinue behind, asking even the chamberlain to depart. His only companion was Bhagurayana. When they were alone, Malayaketu said, 'I don't understand why Bhadrabhatta and the others who crossed to our side from Chandragupta's came to me through our general and not through Rakshasa, who is dearest to me and my most trusted ally.'

Bhagurayana said, 'They had to approach you through someone you trust. Remember, Rakshasa's hostility is towards Chanakya and not Chandragupta. If Chanakya were to fall from favour, then Rakshasa could seek an alliance with Chandragupta. After all, Chandragupta is related to the Nandas. Rakshasa could also help his friends who are in prison. If this were to happen, you would obviously suspect all the men that had come to you through Rakshasa.'

As they approached Rakshasa's rooms, they heard him speaking with someone else. Malayaketu stopped and indicated that he wished to overhear what Rakshasa was saying. 'Did you go to the poet in the city, as I had told you to do?' Rakshasa asked Kabharaka. Kabharaka answered gleefully, 'I did, sir. And gave him your instructions about composing verses that would create mutual suspicion between the king and his minister. Chandragupta had commanded the citizens to celebrate the Kaumudi festival, but Chanakya had rescinded the order. They got into an argument and the king suggested that you were a better minister. And then, he sacked Chanakya as his prime minister!' 'Is that all?' asked Rakshasa anxiously.

Malayaketu whispered, 'Isn't that enough?' Bhaguryana explained, 'This is too small a matter. After all, Chandragupta is a good man. As he is loyal and courteous, he would not turn against Chanakya just for this. Chanakya, too, would not risk alienating the king over something as trivial as a festival celebration. We need something more, a more dangerous betrayal.'

Karabhaka continued, 'There is more, sir. Chandragupta is also not pleased that Chanakya allowed both you and Malayaketu to escape the city without harm!' 'Shakatadasa!' exclaimed Rakshasa to the man who had just entered the room. 'You did this! I have power over Chandragupta now!' 'Sir, Chandanadasa can be freed, you can meet your family again and there is an end to Jivasiddhi's troubles!' Shakatadasa replied.

'What does he mean about Chandragupta?' whispered Malayaketu. 'It means that Chandragupta is no longer the problem,' said Bhaguryana carefully. 'But where is Chanakya?' asked Rakshasa. 'Has he retired to the forest to meditate? It's unthinkable that a man who would not take an insult from the Nandas would give up everything after a quarrel with an upstart like that Maurya!'

'Why is he so interested in Chanakya being in the forest?' asked Malayaketu in hushed tones. 'Ah,' mumbled Bhagurayana. 'He can only achieve his ends when Chanakya is away.'

Rakshasa dismissed Karabhaka and Shakatadasa and said aloud that he wanted to visit Malayaketu. Prince Malayaketu stepped forward as soon as he heard this and was warmly welcomed. 'Our armies are ready to attack,' he said. 'We are just waiting for some indication of vulnerability.' 'There is one,' said Rakshasa. 'There is a rift between Chandragupta and Chanakya!' Malayaketu was not convinced. 'But that leaves Chanakya vulnerable, not Chandragupta. In fact, those whom Chanakya alienated will now love Chandragupta all the more.' 'That may be so, but there are so many more citizens still loyal to the Nandas. They are waiting for you and your armies, they will welcome you and support you. I myself am one of those citizens,' Rakshasa reassured the young prince. 'Chandragupta believes in making decisions along with his ministers. And without Chanakya by his side, he's nothing but a suckling babe! The people will support us – all we need is a word from you!' 'Very well,' said Malayaketu. 'My armies are ready.'

It was now up to Siddharthaka to carry out the task that he had been assigned by Chanakya. As he was on his way to meet Malayaketu, he ran into a monk (who was Jivasiddhi in disguise) who warned him that going in and out of the prince's camp was no longer a simple matter – all those who entered and left had to show some kind of authorization that was stamped with Rakshasa's seal. Bhagurayana was seated in an outside pavilion, providing stamped letters to all those who left the camp. He had started to feel some regret for deceiving young Malayaketu who held him in some affection and obviously trusted him. At the same time, Malayaketu was wondering about Rakshasa. Would he make an alliance with Chandragupta now that Chanakya was gone or, would he stay loyal to Malayaketu and the memory of Parvata?

Soon, Jivasiddhi approached Bhagurayana for permission to enter the camp. 'Off to do Rakshasa's work, are you?' Bhagurayana hailed him. Jivasiddhi did not seem pleased with this jocularity but after some banter, he insinuated that he was displeased with Rakshasa and had valuable information to share. Bhagurayana was persuasive and so, Jivasiddhi told him that when he had lived in Pataliputra, he had been close to Rakshasa. He knew that it was Rakshasa and not Chanakya who had sent the vishakanya to kill Parvata, Malayaketu's father. 'And taking me to be the murderer, Chanakya banished me from the kingdom. Now, Rakshasa is planning to kill me,' said the monk.

Malayaketu stepped forward and the monk realized that he had heard everything for he burst out, 'Rakshasa in name and rakshasa by nature!' Bhagurayana remembered Chanakya's instructions that Rakshasa was to be kept alive at all costs and so he said, placatingly, 'Sit down, prince, and listen to me. In the world of politics, nothing is personal. At the time your father was killed, he was the only obstacle in the way of Rakshasa restoring a Nanda to the throne, for he was stronger than Chandragupta. Rakshasa had to remove him, for he was the greater adversary.' 'You are right,' said Malayaketu. 'Killing Rakshasa may turn people against us and get in the way of our eventual success.'

An attendant came in to announce that the captain of the guard had arrested a man who was carrying a letter and trying to leave the camp without appropriate authorization. Bhagurayana asked for the man to be brought in – it was Siddharthaka. 'I am a servant of Minister Rakshasa,' he said. 'I have been entrusted with a task. I have a letter to deliver, and it carries the minister's personal seal.' 'Read the letter, Bhagurayana,' said Malayaketu. Bhagurayana began to read. 'Salutations from one honourable person to another. The enemy has been removed. It is now time to make an alliance by providing the reward that was promised earlier. It will allow both to help their benefactors. Some want money, others want elephants, still others want land. The three items that were sent have been received. Here is something more, so that the letter does not seem trivial. Take it. Siddharthaka will tell you the rest.' 'What kind of letter is this, Siddharthaka?' asked Bhagurayana. 'I don't know, sir,' came the reply. 'Who are you supposed to give this to?' asked Bhagurayana. 'You, sir! You arrested me!' stammered Siddharathaka. 'Take him away and give him a good beating!' shouted Bhagurayana.

An attendant took the prisoner away but returned very quickly, carrying a box. 'I found this on his person when he was being beaten,' he said, handing it over. 'Careful with the seal, Bhagurayana,' said Malayaketu. 'Open the box and show me what's inside. Aha! This is the very ornament that I gave Rakshasa. I'm sure this letter is intended for Chandragupta.' 'Beat that rascal messenger until he confesses,' ordered Bhagurayana.

The attendant came back shortly with Siddharthaka. 'He wants to tell you everything,' he said. 'Please, sir, promise me safe passage and I will tell you what my mission was,' said Siddharthaka. 'Rakshasa gave me this letter to give to Chandragupta. And here is the clue to understanding the code.' Siddharthaka named five kings from the region around the Maurya territories. 'These are my friends and they have been the first to enter into an alliance with us. One of them wants Malayaketu's wealth, another his elephants, and another his land. They should be given what they asked for so that they can have the same pleasure that I have at besting Chanakya.' 'What?' Malayaketu thought to himself. 'These are the kings that have been my allies. But they are all friends of Rakshasa. I should have known better.' Aloud, he said, 'Bring Minister Rakshasa here!'

Rakshasa was in his own tent, going over the plans he had

made. 'I cannot be at peace as long as there are deserters from Chandragupta's armies in our forces.' He called for his attendant. 'Tell our commanders that it is time for our armies to move forward. This is the formation which they must use – the Khasa and Shabara force in the lead behind me, the Gandharvas and Yavanas holding the middle, the Shakas and Hunas in the rear. The rest, under the command of Kulutu, should form a guard around Prince Malayaketu.' An attendant came in and told Rakshasa that he had been summoned by Malayaketu. 'I cannot go into his presence unadorned,' said Rakshasa, 'for he himself has given me ornaments. Bring me the jewels that were a gift from the prince.' And having put on the ornaments, he went to meet Malayaketu.

The prince apologized for meeting him at such a late hour and then asked about battle formations that Rakshasa had been working on. He noted to himself that the very kings who had been identified as now loyal to Chandragupta were the kings who were to fight closest to him and guard him. He said, 'Why have you sent this fellow here? And what is this letter?' 'Ah, this is Siddharthaka,' said Rakshasa, smiling. 'He told us that you sent him to Chandragupta with this letter and with verbal clues to understanding its code,' said Bhagurayana. 'I was beaten, sir,' cried Siddharthaka. 'I told them what they wanted to hear!' Bhagurayana showed the incriminating letter to Rakshasa together with the ornament that authenticated it. 'This cannot be a fabrication,' said Malayaketu, 'because I know this is the ornament that I gave you. Explain how this could be.' 'This is not an ornament of confirmation,' replied Rakshasa. 'I gave this to Siddharthaka as a gift for all the work he was doing.' 'That's an expensive gift,' retorted Malayaketu. 'But what about the verbal clue that this man is carrying in his head? The letter even has your seal, so don't deny that you wrote it!' 'Anyone can write a letter and copy a seal,' said Rakshasa. Bhagurayana intervened and spoke to Siddharthaka. 'Who wrote this?' 'Shakatadasa!' 'Bring him here,' ordered Malayaketu. 'Sir, in Rakshasa's presence he will never admit to writing this letter,' said Bhagurayana. 'Let us look at another sample of his handwriting and compare the two. And we should also take a look at the signet ring.'

An attendant was sent off to fetch both, and when the new piece of writing was examined, it was identical to that in the letter. As was the signet ring. 'My friend has betrayed me,' thought Rakshasa. 'He is in league with Siddharthaka.' 'And now,' said Malayaketu, 'the letter says you accepted three pieces of jewellery. Is this one of them?' 'I bought this, sir,' said Rakshasa. 'This is my father's ornament,' Malayaketu burst out. 'Where did you get it? I fear that you have gone over to Chandragupta's side, and clearly, these jewels were your price!' Rakshasa knew that he could not deny the letter and that no one would believe him if he said that it was Shakatadasa who was the traitor. 'Fate has turned against me, I have nothing to say,' Rakshasa bowed his head. 'Fate! Fate!' shouted Malayaketu. 'Fate sent the vishakanya to kill my father, fate made my father trust you, fate has let us be defeated by Chandragupta! You are blameless?' 'I did not send the vishakanya to kill your father. I don't know who did,' said Rakshasa quietly. 'Shall we ask the monk, then?' Malayaketu would not be stopped. 'Bhagurayana! Those five kings who have turned against me. Have them burnt alive. The ones who wanted my elephants, let those same elephants trample them! I fight openly, Rakshasa. You can go and debase yourself in front of Chandragupta. Come, let us march on Pataliputra with our armies.' Rakshasa was left alone with his thoughts once more.

In another part of the city, Siddharthaka was making his way to his friend's house. He was in a merry mood after the success of his mission and all the rewards he had received from both Chanakya and the king. His friend embraced him and asked why he was so happy and where he had gotten all his fine clothes and ornaments. 'Listen,' said Siddharthaka with his arm around his friend's shoulder. 'Chanakya manipulated things such that Malayaketu sacked Rakshasa and banished him and had all those rebel kings put to death. And then Rakshasa got the other allies to rise up and capture Malayaketu, who is now a prisoner. What a man!' The friend was surprised. 'But, we heard that it was Chanakya who had been sacked by our king!' 'More fools, you, for believing that!' said Siddharthaka triumphantly. 'So where is Rakshasa now?' the friend asked. 'Oh, he's making his way back to the city, I heard,' Siddharthaka said. 'He's being tailed by Udambara, the master spy. I heard Rakshasa's coming back here to look for his friend Chandanadasa.' 'Will he be saved?' 'No, you and I are supposed to disguise ourselves as executioners and take Rakshasa off to the execution grounds where he is to be impaled! Come on, now. Off we go!'

Elsewhere, a man was waiting with a noose in his hands. 'This noose is strong, like all of Chanakya's skills and strategies, impossible to break,' he said to himself. 'I have reached the place where Udambara said that Rakshasa would come. Here he is, let me hide.' Rakshasa came into sight, walking unsteadily like a man who was lost. He was talking to himself. 'The Goddess of Fortune is so fickle, she is now with Chandragupta, no doubt attracted by his wealth and power. And Fate – what can you say of her! I tried to help the Nanda monarch, I tried to help his son, but nothing works if fate is against you. Now, I will die. I will be dishonoured. That is unbearable, to lose my honour. I have never betrayed anyone – I used to ride here with my king like a king myself and now, look at me, sneaking in like a thief! Let me sit here on the broken stone bench that so resembles my broken fortune. In the distance, I hear the drums that announce the capture of Malayaketu . . . ' Rakshasa sighed and sat down heavily.

The man with the noose saw that his moment had come. 'I must now do as Chanakya instructed,' he said to himself. Then, within sight of Rakshasa, pretending not to notice him, the man placed the noose around his own neck. Rakshasa leapt up from the stone bench and shouted, 'What are you doing, my man? Stop!' 'I have no reason to live, sir. I have lost my dearest friend,' the man replied. 'I am in the same situation,' said Rakshasa. 'Tell me more, if it is not a secret and if it does not increase your pain.' 'No secret at all. My friend was a jeweller, his name was Jishnudasa . . . ' began the man. Rakshasa's heart leapt. 'He must be a friend of Chandanadasa's!' The man continued, 'My friend has a good friend named Chandanadasa. His Majesty pronounced the death sentence on him for sheltering Minister Rakshasa's family. Chandanadasa is to be executed forthwith – my friend offered all his wealth as a ransom for Chandanadasa's life, but the king refused. He said Chandanadasa must die. So, my friend has decided to kill himself and I, who cannot bear to live without him, have also resolved to die.' 'Is Chandanadasa still alive?' Hope sprang up in Rakshasa's heart. 'If he is, I will rescue him and you will be able to prevent your friend from taking his life!' 'Sir, from your words and your grief and your valour, I feel that you must be Rakshasa himself,' said the man. 'I am, indeed, Rakshasa! Now come, let us go rescue our friends!' The man fell at Rakshasa's feet. 'I am blessed, I am blessed to have met you. But you cannot go there waving your sword – the executioners have order to kill Chandanadasa the moment someone tries to save him!' 'Then I shall offer my life in place of his!' said Rakshasa fiercely.

Chandanadasa was being led to the execution grounds, followed by his wife and child and by his friend Jishnudasa. He bid a tearful farewell to his wife and child, urging his wife to stay alive for the sake of their son. Rakshasa burst onto the scene and halted the execution. 'Go and tell your master that I am here, that I offer myself in exchange for my noble friend!' he said to the executioners. While one went off to report to Chanakya, taking Rakshasa with him, the other took Chandanadasa and his family over to sit in the shade of a tree while they waited to hear what would happen next.

Rakshasa was led to Chanakya, who greeted him warmly and reassured him that the 'executioners' were officers of the court and that there was nothing to fear on that account. He also told Rakshasa that Shakatadasa had been deceived into writing the incriminating letter as part of Chanakya's plan and that everything else had also been a series of tricks and deceptions. 'I hope you will forgive me, Minister Rakshasa! These were all part of a political strategy to bring you to Chandragupta. He is waiting to see you.' 'I don't have a choice, do I?' thought Rakshasa to himself. The king entered, and the two men greeted each other with formal civility. 'With Chanakya and Minister Rakshasa by my side, I have nothing to fear,' said the king, smiling. He held out the ceremonial sword of office. 'I do not deserve this,' said Rakshasa. 'If you don't accept it, you cannot save the life of your friend Chandanadasa,' said Chanakya, still playing his cunning game. 'You leave me no choice, then,' said Rakshasa as he took the sword. Chanakya was very pleased with what he had accomplished and presented the new minister to Chandragupta. 'Here he is, Your Majesty! Rakshasa is with us now!' 'And you, Chanakya, you are also with us!' said the king.

An attendant came in to announce that Prince Malayaketu had been brought to the gates by the generals, who were now waiting for further orders. 'Refer the matter to Minister Rakshasa,' said Chanakya. 'These are all things for him to deal with now!' 'Malayaketu has given me shelter,' said Rakshasa without any hesitation. 'He should be set free immediately.' 'Release the prince,' ordered Chanakya. 'Let him and the people know that at the request of Minister Rakshasa, His Majesty Chandragupta has returned his kingdom and all his lands to Malayaketu. Organize a coronation and bring us news. Further, with the minister's advice, the king has appointed the jeweller Chandanadasa as the chief of all the merchant guilds in the city and the kingdom. You can also recall the troops since we have Minister Rakshasa with us, we will not need them anymore.' Chanakya turned to the king. 'Sire, is there anything else that I can do for you?' 'You have given us Minister Rakshasa and the Nandas are no longer of any consequence,' said Chandragupta.

Rakshasa said, 'There is nothing left to do except to ask the gods to give us peace.'

THE LADY WITH THE GARLAND OF JEWELS

BY HARSHA

Harsha pulls this story, too, out of the *Brihatkatha*, but it has a completely different tone and tenor from his *Nagananda*. There is light-heartedness here, as if we already know there will be a happy ending with the lovers reunited and all misunderstandings forgiven, if not forgotten. *Ratnavali* continues the story of King Udayana (who is also the hero of Bhasa's play *Pratijna Yaugandharayanam* in this volume) and his incorrigible palace romances even after he has married Vasavadatta, who is now his chief queen. The play also resembles Kalidasa's *Malavikagnimitra* in that the king falls in love with one of his wife's attendants, who has newly arrived to join her entourage. The high-born young woman must keep her true identity a secret for her own safety. The king's brahmin companion, Vasantaka, plays a crucial role, first in Udayana's seduction of Ratnavali and later, in smoothing Vasavadatta's ruffled feathers.

The *Brihatkatha*, as a source text for these plays, was preceded by other similar story collections and concerns itself not with the gods but with the trials and triumphs of humans and vidyadharas, a class of celestial beings who knew magic and could fly through the air. Vidyadharas appear in the myths and tales of Buddhists, Jains and Hindus alike, which could explain the multi-religious universe reflected in these stories.

List of Important Characters

Kanchanamala – Queen Vasavadatta's favourite attendant
Ratnavali – Simhala princess who joins Queen Vasavadatta's retinue
Susangata – young attendant
Udayana – king of Kosambi
Vasantaka – Udayana's companion and close friend
Vasavadatta – Udayana's chief queen
Vikramabahu – Simhala king and Queen Vasavadatta's uncle
Yaugandharayana – Udayana's chief minister

PROLOGUE

King Udayana was the ruler of Kosambi. He was married to the beautiful queen Vasavadatta, whom he loved very much. Yaugandharayana was the king's minister. He was devoted to the king and used his many powers and abilities to make sure that the king was successful in all that he did.

Yaugandharayana had been told of a prophecy that concerned the king – if Udayana were to marry the Simhala princess, Ratnavali (the Lady with the Garland of Jewels), he would become a powerful emperor who would bring many lands under his control. Yaugandharayana wanted nothing more than this, so he sent the Simhala king, Vikramabahu, a proposal for a marriage between Udayana and Ratnavali.

But as Vikramabahu was Vasavadatta's uncle, he knew that Udayana loved Vasavadatta deeply and he was reluctant to send his daughter into a situation where she would be unhappy. So, he hesitated. But while the messenger with the proposal was still at Udayana's court, the news arrived that Queen Vasavadatta had been killed in a fire. This was not true. It was merely a ploy by the clever minister to secure Ratnavali's hand for Udayana. But Ratnavali's father, not knowing the true story, put his daughter on a ship and sent her off with his blessings.

When the travellers were on the open seas, a great storm arose and their ship was wrecked. Ratnavali managed to hold onto a floating plank of wood and was rescued by merchants who were on their way to Kosambi. From her clothes and her jewellery, they recognized her as a woman of noble birth, but Ratnavali did not wish to say who she really was because she did not want to be held for ransom by the men who had rescued her. So, she pretended to have lost her memory. When they reached Kosambi, the merchants quickly handed Ratnavali over to the courtiers of the palace. Yaugandharayana recognized her from the garland of jewels that she was wearing and, to further his scheme of getting her married to the king, he told Queen Vasavadatta to keep the unfortunate girl as a maid. He introduced her as Sagarika (the Lady of the Ocean). He also saw this as a chance to get the queen accustomed to the idea of a second wife for Udayana.

Standing in his balcony with his friend Vasantaka, King Udayana was enjoying the festival of the God of Love as the citizens celebrated with singing and dancing, wearing garlands of leaves and flowers. Red powder filled the air as if a second dawn was rising over the city. There was music and laughter everywhere – people sprayed each other with coloured water and shared fruits and sweets and other delicacies. Two of the queen's maids came to the balcony and took Vasantaka away to join the dancing. Then, they remembered that they had a message for the king, and they came back to him, giggling. 'The queen asks you to meet her near the ashoka tree in the grove where she will be performing the ritual for the God of Love,' they said shyly. 'Tell the queen I shall be there,' said Udayana happily. Accompanied by Vasantaka, the king wandered through the gardens, enjoying the gentle breeze that carried the scent of flowers and listening to sweet birdsong and the humming of the bees.

Queen Vasavadatta entered the garden from the other side and began to make her way to the shrine where she wanted to perform the ritual. She was accompanied by her maids, including the new girl, Sagarika, who had just joined her retinue. As Sagarika moved forward to place the flowers and other offerings at the base of the shrine, the queen was struck by an uncomfortable thought. 'Oh dear! This girl will be seen by the very person that I've been hiding her from! I think it's best to send her back into the palace, safe from wandering eyes!' She called out to Sagarika and said sharply, 'What are you doing here? You've left our mynah bird unattended, poor thing. Go back and take care of it immediately!' Sagarika replied that she would but in her heart she was resentful, because she wanted to watch the ceremonies and rituals in this land that was not her own. 'That silly bird is hardly alone, the palace is full of people,' she thought. 'I'm going to hide here and see if their ceremonies are any different from the ones we perform in my father's kingdom.'

Udayana entered the grove with Vasantaka and was warmly greeted by the queen and her attendants. The queen began the worship of the bodiless God of Love by anointing the bark of the ashoka tree with auspicious vermillion powder. Her graceful movements enhanced her beauty and her delicate, slim figure. The king's eyes filled with love as he watched her and he was well pleased when she turned to honour him with flowers and fragrant oils in her hand.

Sagarika had finished gathering flowers for herself and returned to her hiding place near the grove just in time to see Vasavadatta honouring the king. 'Look! They honour the God of Love himself! He is here in person!' she thought. 'At home, we honour an image of this bodiless god in a painting.' In the distance, the royal herald announced the end of the day and invited all the people to pay homage to King Udayana. 'Oh, goodness,' Sagarika was startled. 'This is the king, the very one that my father wanted me to marry. I never imagined that any man could be this handsome!' She realized that the royal party was moving back to the palace, and she hurried away so that she could be back before the queen arrived.

Some days later, another young maid named Susangata was looking for Sagarika, who was nowhere to be found. A courtier directed her to the banana grove saying she had seen Sagarika walking there, that she had seemed morose and that she was carrying a painting board and paints. Sagarika set down her board and paints in the grove and prayed to the God of Love for a glimpse of her new beloved. 'If I can't see him any other way, I shall have to be satisfied with this,' she sobbed and started to paint a picture of the handsome man she had seen the day before. Susangata crept up behind her and watched quietly. Suddenly, she burst out, 'Why, that's the king! I didn't know that you could paint so well. Let me see – but who have you painted him as?' Sagarika blushed. 'As the God of Love,' she replied. 'That's clever,' said Susangata. 'There's something missing though. Let me fill it in.' She took the paints and brushes and started to add to the picture. 'Look, I've painted the God of Love with his wife Rati.' 'That's not Rati,' cried Sagarika. 'That's me! You've put me in the picture with the king! Oh, what shall I do?' she wailed. 'I am in love with the most unattainable person!' 'Don't be embarrassed,' Susangata comforted her friend. 'It's natural for someone as beautiful as you to be attracted to more beauty. Your secret is safe with me, though I do worry about this little mynah that has been listening to us. I hope she hasn't picked up enough to spill the story to others. But, you look like you're about to faint. Let me fetch some cooling lotus leaves, they will help to calm you.'

In the distance, a voice called out, 'A monkey has escaped his golden chains and has run amok inside the palace. Courtiers are fleeing in all directions! There is much confusion! Beware, beware!' The two young women lifted their skirts and ran from the grove, going deeper into the banana plantation. 'I've left the paint board in the grove. We have to go back,' cried Sagarika. 'Leave it!' said Susangata as she grabbed Sagarika's hand. 'That wicked monkey has opened the bird cage and the mynah has flown away. We need to get her back before she repeats everything that she heard us say!' They ran after the bird.

Udayana and Vasantaka came into the grove, talking excitedly about a holy man who had the power to make plants flower in any season. Suddenly, Vasantaka stopped. 'I'm not going any further,' he said firmly. 'What's the matter?' said the king. 'There's a ghost in that tree!' Vasantaka was now trembling with fear. 'Nonsense, our garden has no ghosts!' said Udayana. 'Listen, listen,' said Vasantaka, clutching the king's arm. 'Can't you hear him babbling . . . ' 'That's a bird, Vasantaka, a mynah,' laughed the king. 'Let's listen to what she's saying.' The men listened carefully and the bird repeated the conversation between Sagarika and Susangata. They learned that some young woman, deeply in love, had painted a picture of her beloved and that she pined for him to the point of making herself unwell. She had no hope for her relationship because he was so very far above her in social status and so, she was prepared to die. The men laughed at the lover's predicament, but they had become completely involved in the story. They heard that the young woman's friend had added her to the picture in order to tease her.

Suddenly, without warning, the bird flew away. Determined to learn more, they ran behind her and stumbled into the banana grove. On the grass, near a marble bench, lay a painting board. Vasantaka picked it up. 'What have we here?' he shouted to the king. 'Why, it's a picture of you portrayed as the God of Love!' 'Show me,' said the king. But Vasantaka moved away and said, teasingly, 'Aha, you are not the only one in the picture, there is a beautiful girl next to you. I wonder why she's so pale and sad . . . ' Udayana gave Vasantaka a rich bracelet that he was wearing as a bribe in exchange for the painting.

Meanwhile, Sagarika and Susangata had also reached the banana grove in their quest for the talkative bird. When they heard men's voices, they hid themselves. They heard the king say, 'This young woman is so lovely!' Susangata giggled and nudged Sagarika. 'It seems the king likes you,' she whispered. The king continued to gaze at the painting and spoke eloquently and at length about the beauty of the woman in it. He imagined the woman who had painted him crying over her unrequited love. He pictured her embracing the image of himself, imagining how her body must have ached with love and desire.

Susangata thought things had gone too far and that the king might be losing his mind. She burst into the grove. Vasantaka recognized her as the queen's maid and tried to hide the painting, but Susangata had already told the king that she had overheard his conversation with Vasantaka and that she had noted his appreciation of the young woman in the painting.

The king took off his earrings and placed them in Susangata's hand. 'Take these,' he said. 'There's no need for the queen to know any of this.' 'I only came to take you to the woman in the painting,' smiled Susangata. 'Her name is Sagarika and she's annoyed that I added her to the picture. You could make her feel better.' She led Udayana and Vasantaka to where Sagarika was. 'Oh, oh!' Sagarika said to herself when she saw the king, the object of her heart's desire. 'What am I to do now, what should I say, how should I act?' Vasantaka broke out in praise of the young woman. 'My, my! I have never seen such beauty, such grace, such flawless skin, such a slim waist, such generous hips . . . what do you think, My Lord,' he said, turning to the king. The king, too, was full of praise for Sagarika.

Sagarika was mortified and said to her friend, 'Is this the painting board you have brought back!' 'She is still angry, Your Majesty,' said Susangata to the king. 'Perhaps you can take her hand and change her mood.' Sagarika trembled at the touch of the king's hand, but she was not appeased. 'Come, come,' said the king. 'Who can continue to be angry with a friend who loves them and acts for their benefit?' Vasantaka interrupted their conversation with an urgent whisper. 'It's Queen Vasavadatta!' Susangata pulled Sagarika away from the king and the young women ran from the grove. 'Quick, Vasantaka, hide the picture!' said the king, greatly agitated. Vasantaka hid the painting under his clothes.

The queen entered the grove with her retinue of maids and was pleasantly surprised to see her husband. 'How nice that you are here! I wanted to view the new jasmine creeper with you, but from the flush on your face, it would seem that you have already seen it,' she teased. Vasantaka grew nervous and the painting slipped out from where he had concealed it. Kanchanamala, the queen's favourite maid, picked it up and said eagerly, 'Let's see who's in the painting!' The queen took the painting from her. 'Why, this is my husband!' she said. 'And surely this is Sagarika.' She smiled as she turned to Udayana, but behind the smile, she was seething. 'Who made this painting, husband dear?' she said sweetly. Vasantaka jumped in to the conversation. 'Madam, this is nothing to remark on. I mentioned how difficult it is to draw one's own self and the king did a painting to show me his skills! That's all!' 'And this girl in the picture? Did you paint her, Vasantaka?' asked the queen, smiling no longer. 'My dear, do not be concerned. This is some girl that I drew from my imagination. I have never laid eyes on anyone who looked like this,' stammered the king. Kanchanamala whispered to the queen, 'That could be, madam.

Such coincidences are known to happen.' 'You are a fool!' said the queen sharply. 'I don't trust anything that Vasantaka says!' She turned to her husband. 'I have a headache. I'm going back to my chambers,' she said curtly. The king clutched at her skirt, pleading, 'What can I say? If I say, don't be angry, it would be wrong because you are not angry. If I say, I won't do it again, it would mean I was guilty. If I say, this is not my fault, it would be a lie. My dear one, what can I possibly say to you?' The queen pulled her skirt away from him and said, 'You imagine things. All I have is a headache.' She left with her maids following behind. Vasantaka heaved a sigh of relief. 'Saved!' he muttered. 'You know nothing,' said the king sadly. 'You didn't notice that Vasavadatta was hiding her anger and her sadness. I saw tears in her eyes. She is too well brought up to show her true feelings.'

The next day, Vasantaka summoned Susangata. He told her that the king was unwell and that the only cure for his condition was a meeting with Sagarika. Susangata said that she would dress Sagarika in the queen's clothes and ornaments, that she herself would dress as Kanchanamala, and that the king should meet them by the flowering jasmine creeper in the garden. Kanchanamala had been sent to inquire after the king's health, so she overheard the conversation between Vasantaka and Susangata. She could not wait to tell the queen about the deceit that was being planned.

Meanwhile, Udayana moped around like a lovesick teenager. His body was hot with desire, and his heart overflowed with love for Sagarika, but it beat faster with fear for her since she had angered the queen. Vasantaka told Udayana about the clever plan he had hatched for him to meet his beloved. The king was so pleased he pulled off one of his bracelets and handed it to his friend. 'My wife will love this, she loves gold,' smiled Vasantaka to himself. As the sun was setting, Udayana and Vasantaka made their way to the garden to keep their appointment. Udayana settled down by the flowering creeper and Vasantaka went to fetch Sagarika, who would be dressed as the queen. But Kanchanamala, who had told Vasavadatta about the plan, was now leading her to the picture gallery where Sagarika was waiting to be taken to Udayana. Vasantaka was already at the picture gallery and when he saw Kanchanamala and Vasavadatta, he assumed that the two ladies were Sagarika and Susangata, in disguise as the queen and her maid as they had planned.

With great haste, Vasantaka led the women to where the king was moaning and sighing, impatient to see Sagarika. The moment Udayana saw Vasavadatta, he came close to her whispering, 'Sagarika, O Sagarika!' over and over again. 'Look, my love,' he said, pointing to the moon. 'The moon is pale compared to you. You have robbed the moon of all its loveliness!' Vasavadatta had run out of patience and the game of double deceit was not amusing her any more. She pulled off her veil and said, 'Sagarika! Sagarika! What Sagarika? I am Vasavadatta, your queen!' 'Oh, my dearest darling!' cried Udayana as he knelt before her. 'Please forgive me . . . ' 'Nonsense! All these dears and darlings are not for me, they are for Sagarika. I'm leaving!' Vasavadatta stomped off in tears of rage. 'Oh, no!' said the king. 'She has left without forgiving me! What shall I do now?' 'Think of poor Sagarika,' said Vasantaka. 'What will the queen do to her?' 'Come on, let's find Vasavadatta and calm her down!' said Udayana.

They hurried towards the garden entrance. But Sagarika, dressed as the queen, had arrived, murmuring to herself that the queen had found out all about the plan. 'There is nothing left for me to do but hang myself. This disgrace is too much to bear!' She started toward the ashoka tree. Vasantaka and Udayana heard her footsteps and stopped in their tracks. 'I think the queen is coming back,' whispered Vasantaka. 'I knew it,' said the king happily. 'I knew she would forgive me!' Vasantaka crept through the bushes and saw Sagarika placing a noose of flowers and vines around her neck. 'O my goodness,' cried Vasantaka. 'The queen is preparing to hang herself!' The king rushed forward and embraced the weeping young woman, who said over and over again, 'Let me go, let me go! Sagarika is but a poor slave girl. She must die . . . ' Udayana recognized her voice. He was overjoyed and placed Sagarika's arms around his neck. 'Ah, my sweet girl!'

Elsewhere in the palace, Vasavadatta was regretting her hasty actions with the king, for she really did love him. 'I was cruel to him,' she said to Kanchanamala. 'He begged my pardon, he fell at my feet. I really should forgive him. Look, here he comes! I'm going to surprise him from behind.' As Vasavadatta approached Udayana quietly, she heard him talking to Sagarika. 'How could you treat me like this?' he sighed. 'You are so heartless!' 'Your sweet words are only for your wife, the queen,' wept Sagarika. 'She is cold and cruel,' said Udayana. 'I begged for her forgiveness and she walked away without a second look. That can't be love. It's you that makes my heart leap!'

Vasavadatta stepped out of her hiding place. 'What a love scene this is!' she said sarcastically. 'Dear wife, this is not what you think, I didn't mean a word of what I said,' stammered Udayana. Vasantaka broke into the conversation. 'My Lady,' he said, quaking. 'I thought she was you from the clothes that she's wearing. And I did think that you were trying to hang yourself after what had happened. And so, I called the king to save your life. Look at this noose!' he said, holding it out to Vasavadatta.

'You should put that noose around your own neck you fool!' she snapped. 'And as for that silly girl, you wait and see what I have in store for her! Kanchanamala, take them away!' The queen marched off behind her maid and the two captives.

Sometime later, Vasantaka was on his way home, very pleased with himself. He was admiring the new clothes and ornaments the queen had given him. 'All's well, all's well,' he said to himself. The king has appeased the queen and the queen has filled my stomach with rich and delicious foods.' Suddenly, he came upon Susangata, crying as if her heart would break. 'Oh, poor Sagarika,' she wept. 'Who knows what will happen to her now! She gave me this wonderful garland of jewels and when I said I didn't want it, she told me to give it some brahmin as charity.' She looked up and saw Vasantaka. 'You are a brahmin,' she said, wiping her eyes. 'Here, take this.' Vasantaka took it eagerly but then he said, 'This is not an ordinary necklace, Susangata. This has to have come from some royal family. I had better take it to the king.'

He found the king in the crystal room of the palace, sitting sadly on his throne. 'I have managed to pacify the queen,' said the king. 'Her own tears dissolved her anger. But now, ah, my sweet Sagarika! And my dear friend, Vasantaka! Both taken from me so hastily!' 'Sire! I am here!' shouted Vasantaka. Udayana hugged him and asked, 'But what has happened to that lovely girl, my Sagarika?' Vasantaka hung his head. 'Susangata told me that the queen sent her off to who knows where. And she gave me this necklace that Sagarika gave her.' He held the garland of jewels out to the king. 'What use are these cold gems when I long for her warm arms,' cried the king.

They were interrupted by an announcement that proclaimed the victory of Udayana's armies against distant Kosala. In that mood of celebration, Vasavadatta joined Udayana in the crystal room, promising him great entertainment by a famous magician. Following on the heels of the military messengers came a courtier saying that the minister and the chamberlain of the Simhala kingdom had arrived. With some hesitation, they told the king what they believed to be true – that King Vikramabahu had pledged his daughter, Ratnavali, to King Udayana when he learned that Queen Vasavadatta had been killed in a palace fire, but then Ratnavali had been drowned in a shipwreck . . . Vasavadatta burst out laughing when she heard them talk about the palace fire, and even King Udayana was having trouble following the story. The Simhala men continued and said that it was all their fault that Ratnavali had died because they were the ones escorting her. At that moment, a huge commotion broke out – 'Fire! Fire!' someone shouted. 'A fire in the palace!' Vasavadatta leapt up from her seat. 'Save her, please save her! I have put Sagarika in chains in the dungeon! Oh, that poor child . . . ' Before anyone could stop him, Udayana ran out in search of Sagarika. When he found her, he lifted her into his arms and then, he noticed that there was neither fire nor flames nor smoke. 'What is this?' he said, looking around, unable to understand what was happening. Just then, he saw Vasavadatta. And the Simhala ministers. And then, Vasantaka. 'Am I dreaming,' he asked. 'Where is the fire?' 'There is no fire,' said Vasantaka. 'It was all the sorcerer's trick!'

The men from the Simhala court were whispering to each other. 'Could this be Ratnavali?' they said when they saw the girl that the king had rescued from the dungeon. 'That necklace we saw, it's the same . . . ' 'Who is this lady?' asked the chamberlain. 'Our minister, Yaugandharayana, left her with me, saying that she was a child of the sea,' said Vasavadatta. 'Ratnavali!' shouted the minister. 'Good minister of my father's court!' cried Ratnavali. 'Ratnavali? My cousin?' Vasavadatta moved forward to embrace the young woman. 'The princess of Simhala?' said the bewildered king. 'Here, take this back,' said Vasantaka, placing the garland of jewels around Ratnavali's neck. 'Don't cry, child,' said Vasavadatta to Ratnavali, 'it's all over now.' She turned to Udayana. 'Dear husband, forgive me. I didn't know. Yaugandharayana told me nothing.' Yaugandharayana finally spoke. 'This is all my doing, Sire,' he said to the king. 'Once Queen Vasavadatta had come to terms with you taking a second wife, I knew that I had to act quickly. I had heard that when Ratnavali, princess of the Simhala kingdom was just a child, a great sage had predicted that whoever married her would rule the world. But her father would not give her to you in marriage because of Queen Vasavadatta. He did not want either his daughter or his niece to be unhappy with a rival wife. So, I started the rumour that the queen had died in a palace fire. The news reached the Simhala kingdom and then . . . ' 'The rest we know,' said the king. 'But why did you give Sagarika – I mean Ratnavali – to my wife?' 'So that you would see her and fall in love with her,' replied Yaugandharayana, chuckling. 'Yes, I did all this. I even arranged the sorcerer! Now, it's all up to Queen Vasavadatta.' 'You mean, I should bestow this lovely girl on my husband,' said Vasavadatta. She adorned Ratnavali with jewels and took her by the hand. 'We are more than cousins now, we are sisters! Sire, look after her. She is alone and far from her people. Ratnavali, be a worthy queen to this good king!'

Yaugandharayana had the last word. 'Ratnavali is with us, Vasavadatta is happy, Kosala has been conquered, King Udayana is on the throne. I could not have done better!'